LITERATURE IN CHRISTIAN PERSPECTIVE

Other titles in the series:

SERIES EDITORS: Leslie J Francis and Jeff Astley

LITERATURE IN CHRISTIAN PERSPECTIVE

Becoming Faithful Readers

Bridget Nichols

DARTON · LONGMAN + TODD

First published in 2000 by
Darton, Longman and Todd Ltd
1 Spencer Court
140-142 Wandsworth High Street
London SW18 4JJ

ISBN 0-232-52379-7

A catalogue record for this book is available from the British Library.

Designed by Sandie Boccacci
Phototypeset in Minion by Intype London Ltd
Printed and bound in Great Britain by
Page Bros, Norwich, Norfolk

CONTENTS

ACKNOWLEDGEMENTS

I should like to thank the following publishers for allowing me to reprint material:

The General Synod of the Anglican Church in Aotearoa, New Zealand and Polynesia for permission to use their text of the Benedicite Aotearoa; the Marvell Press, England and Australia, for permission to reprint 'Myxomatosis' by Philip Larkin from *The Less Deceived*; Faber and Faber for permission to reprint 'Aubade' by Philip Larkin from his *Collected Poems*.

The following publishers have kindly allowed me to quote from published works:

HarperCollins from *The Gate of Angels* by Penelope Fitzgerald; William Heinemann from J B Priestley's *An Inspector Calls*.

Gordon Jackson generously made his work available for quotation, and I am particularly grateful to him for the use of Sonnet XV from his *25 Domestic Sonnets*, and lines from his long poem, *Charnal Supper*.

A special debt of gratitude is due to Jeff Astley, whose encouragement, editorial advice, ready wit and endless patience have made this project sustainable.

Quotations from Scripture are all from *The Revised English Bible*, unless otherwise indicated.

PREFACE

At the beginning of the third millennium a new mood is sweeping through the Christian Churches. This mood is reflected in a more radical commitment to discipleship among a laity who wish to be theologically informed and fully equipped for Christian ministry in the secular world.

Exploring Faith: theology for life is designed for people who want to take Christian theology seriously. Taken seriously, Christian theology engages the mind, involves the heart, and seeks active expression in the way we live. Those who explore their faith in this way are beginning to shape a theology for life.

Exploring Faith: theology for life is rooted in the individual experience of the world and in the ways through which God is made known in the world. Such experience is related to and interpreted in the light of the Christian tradition. Each volume in the series takes a key aspect of theology, and explores this aspect in dialogue with the readers' own experience. Each volume is written by a scholar who has clear authority in the area of theology discussed and who takes seriously the ways in which busy adults learn.

The volumes are suitable for all those who wish to learn more about the Christian faith and ministry, including those who have already taken Christian basic courses (such as *Alpha* and *Emmaus*) and have been inspired to undertake further study, those preparing to take theology as an undergraduate course, and those already engaged on degree programmes. The volumes have been developed for individuals to work on alone or for groups to study together.

Already groups of Christians are using the *Exploring Faith: theology for life* series throughout the United Kingdom, linked by an exciting initiative pioneered jointly by the Anglican dioceses, the Board of Education of the Church and World Division and the Ministry Division of the Archbishops' Council of the Church of England, the National Society and the Church Colleges. Used in this way each volume can earn credits towards one of the Church Colleges' Certificates and provide access to degree level study. Further information about the Church Colleges' Certificate Programme is provided on page 126.

The Church Colleges' Certificate Programme integrates well with the lifelong learning agenda which now plays such a crucial role in educational priorities. Learning Christians can find their way into degree-bearing programmes through this series *Exploring Faith: theology for life* linked with the Church Colleges' Certificates.

This series of books originated in materials developed by and for the Aston Training Scheme. Thanks are due to former staff of the Scheme, and in particular to Roger Spiller who conceived of and commissioned the original series, and to Nicola Slee who edited the original materials. In the light of the closure of Aston, this series represents something of the ongoing contribution of the Scheme to the life of the Church.

In preparing a series of this kind, much work is done behind the scenes. Financial and staff support have been generously given by the Ministry Division. Thanks are due to Marilyn Parry for the vision of bringing together the Aston materials and the Anglican Church Colleges of Higher Education. We are also grateful for financial support from the following Church Colleges: Chester College; Christchurch University College, Canterbury; The College of St Mark & St John, Plymouth; St Martin's College, Lancaster; Trinity College Carmarthen; and Whitelands College (Roehampton Institute). Without the industry, patience, perception, commitment and skill of Ruth Ackroyd this series would have remained but a dream.

The series editors wish to express their personal thanks to colleagues who have helped them shape the series identity, especially Diane Drayson, Evelyn Jackson and Katie Worrall, and to the individual authors who have produced high quality text on schedule and so generously accepted firm editorial direction. The editorial work has been supported by the North of England Institute for Christian Education and the Centre for Ministry Studies at the University of Wales, Bangor.

Leslie J Francis
Jeff Astley

INTRODUCTION

The written word, in some form or other, is part of life. Whether we choose our reading principally from works acclaimed for their style, descriptive qualities, narrative technique or power to give us new insights into our own situation in the world, or from the random array of second-hand books at a market stall, or from a daily newspaper, we are all engaged in the business of reading. This never takes place in isolation. We bring with us a number of formative experiences and our involvement in other habitual activities. If we have inherited a tradition of faith, we bring that too.

This book tries to establish a way of connecting the experience of readers of literature who have inherited a particular cultural tradition, with the same group's experience as followers of a particular tradition of faith. In straightforward terms, it sets out to involve its readers in a conversation between the creative forms of poetry, fiction and drama, and the experience and practice of Christian faith. If that aim seems intimidating, then users should be reassured that this is a conversation that can be entered at many levels. The chapters are planned in a way that tries as far as possible to draw students who are new to both theological discussion and critical reading into a very practical dialogue between their own experience and some of the ways of representing experience in literature.

In planning the shape and content of the discussion in the following chapters, I have imagined readers who have:
- some knowledge of Christian faith and practice;
- some acquaintance with the Bible, both Old and New Testaments;
- a curiosity about literature in its various forms;
- an openness to the beauty of language and the sort of creative acts that are possible in language;
- a readiness to be led through reading to new forms of discovery;
- a willingness to revisit the stories of the inheritance of faith through sensitive and alert attention to other kinds of literature.

These imaginary readers are not sophisticated literary critics or trained theologians. Perhaps they have much in common with some of the most interesting and adventurous students I have encountered – the young man who returned to education and trained as a teacher after years working in a shipyard and then running a greengrocer's business, or the former policeman whose joy in discovering his ability to interpret poetry transformed the reading process for an entire class. They might not admit to knowing much about the vocabulary that describes literary techniques, but they will be open to learning how to identify and describe examples they have recognised in ordinary speech or in reading the Bible.

This means that they will engage seriously with the tasks that the exercises invite them to undertake. Here I must emphasise that there is no substitute for reading a text, and reading it more than once. While each chapter encourages readers to focus their attention on key elements in a story, poem or play, it never offers a complete account of a text. That would be an irresponsible claim even for a specialist study. For that reason, each chapter expects that students will already have thought carefully about the material it invites them to explore, and that they will bring their responses to meet the chapter's guidelines for reflection.

Further reading and background

You will find three kinds of further help to pursue interests that may have grown in the course of working through this book. At the end of each chapter, there is a short list of *Further reading*. This includes critical discussions that can help you to engage in something like a dialogue with others who have thought about the material you are reading. It also suggests reference books that can often answer the questions that lie in the background of all the discussions, for example histories of biblical characters or events, unfamiliar literary terms, or technicalities of Christian worship. The list of *References* at the end of the book includes the titles of all critical works mentioned in individual chapters. The *Glossary and biography* provides a checklist of unfamiliar terminology used in the course of chapters, and gives brief information about some of the writers whose work you will encounter.

A foundation library

To make proper preparation possible, I have chosen texts which are not only rich in their potential to open up issues of faith, but also widely available in modestly priced editions and in public libraries. Second-hand bookshops are often a rewarding source of supply.

The following titles will be essential preliminary equipment to accompany the chapters:

- a modern translation of the Bible, for example *The New Revised Standard Version* or *The Revised English Bible*;
- **for chapter 4:** the Collected Works of Shakespeare (there are many inexpensive options) *or* an edition of Shakespeare's *Pericles*, which might be D DelVecchio and A Hammond (eds) (1998), *Pericles* (New Cambridge Shakespeare), Cambridge, Cambridge University Press; or P Edwards (ed.) (1976), *Pericles* (New Penguin Shakespeare), Harmondsworth, Penguin; or F D Hoeniger (ed.) (1997), *Pericles* (The Arden Shakespeare), London, Thomas Nelson;
- **for chapter 7:** an edition of the short stories of Oscar Wilde, such as I Murray (ed.) (1998), *Oscar Wilde: complete shorter fiction* (Oxford World's Classics), Oxford, Oxford University Press; or O Wilde (1994), *The Happy Prince and Other Stories* (Penguin Popular Classics), London, Puffin;
- **for chapter 8:** a modern translation of William Langland, *The Vision of Piers Plowman*, preferably W Langland (1966), *Piers the Ploughman*, tr. J F Goodridge, Harmondsworth, Penguin;
- also **for chapter 8:** a copy of J B Priestley's *An Inspector Calls*, for example the text in J B Priestley (1969), *Time and the Conways and Other Plays*, Harmondsworth, Penguin;
- **for chapter 9:** an edition of Milton, *Paradise Lost* such as J Milton (1998), *Complete Poems*, ed. J Leonard, London, Penguin; or J Milton (1998), *Paradise Lost*, ed. A Fowler, London, Longman; or J Milton, (1998), *Paradise Lost*, ed. C Ricks, London, Penguin;
- **for chapter 10:** Penelope Fitzgerald (1991), *The Gate of Angels*, London, Flamingo.

The principle has been to start with shorter texts. This is to enable students to keep abreast of reading. Proper preparation will enable you to get much more out of each reading exercise, and will help you read ahead in advance of later chapters. With that proviso, the chapters need not necessarily be followed in the sequence in which they appear. Each of them is a self-contained study, although students are encouraged to remember that any new terms, techniques, or insights are not restricted to single instances. Skills taught in one exercise are taught with a view to applying them to other acts of reading.

Aims and ambitions

To say that this book has a goal or aim would in many ways be a denial of what it hopes to achieve. In choosing material, I have tried to act as an introduction agency, with the hope that more meetings with more texts will take place once readers have begun to gain a flavour of a variety of literature. An important part of the planning has been a determination to increase the audience's confidence in their abilities as readers and interpreters.

The overriding ambition of the book might be put like this: by introducing students to a way of bringing their faith to their reading, and their developing skills as readers to the issues raised by faith, it tries to set them on a continuing journey of discovery. This may lead to more specialised studies in areas of literature or theology. On the other hand, it may simply encourage its users to be 'faithful readers' in the very richest sense that term implies.

1. MAPPING THE FIELD

Desert island books

A long-running BBC radio programme asks its celebrity guests to name, among other things, the book they would take if marooned on a desert island. The rules of the game state that the Bible and Shakespeare will be provided. After that, the players have to justify their choice of other reading material to sustain them during their separation from bookshops and libraries. This most often takes the form of works that have made such a powerful impression on their readers that they have returned to them again and again.

Reflecting on experience
Have you played this desert island game, either with other people or in your own imagination? You might have produced a variant version, such as deciding what book you would rescue if your house were on fire.

Recall your choices, and try to express your reasons for choosing one book in particular. Why did you feel that book was essential to your survival?

The game is underpinned by large and fascinating assumptions. It takes for granted that participants will know enough about Shakespeare and the Bible to find them indispensable. This, in turn, implies that most people who are likely to be involved will have a stake in the inheritance of the Judaeo-Christian tradition and the tradition of western literature. The game also tacitly encourages players to select an accompanying book which, even if it does not stand in the classical canon of great works, will nevertheless have a claim to intellectual respectability. It does not expect, for example, that anyone would want to spend many months re-reading a pot-boiler hospital romance. But neither the interviewer nor the listeners would be surprised if the week's guest expressed a wish to have one of Jane Austen's novels as a companion through the period of isolation.

The castaway's library, then, has clear starting points. These represent very broadly what people might be expected to know because they belong to a particular cultural community.

Faith and reading

This book works from similar starting points in its choice of texts for study, but with a strategic purpose. I have imagined an audience of people who wish to place their interest in literature in the light of Christian faith. Some of them might be returning to the activity of reading critically with a relatively recent interest in questions of faith. Others might come equipped with a lifetime of Christian practice, but little exposure to a range of literary works. Others will fall into groups that combine features of both these descriptions.

In all cases, I have counted on a certain amount of preliminary knowledge. So, for example, the discussion in the following chapters takes it for granted that readers will be familiar with the concept of the biblical canon, the events in the narrative of salvation, and the gospels as an account of Jesus' earthly ministry. It also hopes that readers may have met Shakespearean drama and become acquainted with forms of poetry and the novel. Much of this knowledge will have been gathered through schooling and churchgoing and perhaps through exposure to theatre, cinema and televised costume drama.

EXERCISE

Do you recognise yourself in any of the portraits of imaginary readers in the last paragraph? If not, add your particular starting point and background to this gallery. Then spend some time thinking about what you hope to gain from the programme of reading that this book offers.

You may find it useful to keep a note of your expectations, so that you can return to them when you have worked through the readings and exercises that follow.

One of the factors that may have shaped your interest in the meeting of literature with issues of faith is a sense of entering into a conversation with certain poems, novels, plays or prayers. This may have led to a sustaining relationship offering intellectual and spiritual nourishment, and you will probably have gone back to the text again and again. If it was a poem or prayer, you may even have learned it by heart. In the terms of our initial example, this is the text that would have accompanied you to a desert island.

Another factor might have been the nature of the conversation itself. Reading engages us at a number of levels. We might begin simply with the challenge of comprehension, pausing to wonder what a line or a passage means. Events may move us to tears and laughter, and we will want to know the reason for this. Later on, we may question the behaviour of individual characters and their treatment of one another. In the same way, we may feel that the fate of characters is governed unjustly by forces beyond their control. This is a developing pattern of involvement that grows into ethical enquiries about motives, rights and wrongs. Readers who bring Christian faith with them will often find that they have to reassess their commitments of belief in the light of these questions. Sometimes, that process will lead into enquiries about the dealings of God (or fate or destiny, if religious language seems inappropriate) with human beings.

The possibilities I have just described give the impression that every act of reading also calls upon an examination of faith. A claim like this is obviously too broad to pass without further explanation. For one thing, it raises questions about how we read. We are trained to expect that certain works – the Bible, or meditations on aspects of faith or Scripture, or the writings of the medieval mystics – will have an immediate message to convey. Clearly, though, we do not approach every encounter with the printed word anticipating that it will result in new insights into the nature of belief. There is no reason, for example, why a novel by Charles Dickens should be expected to present an explicit theological argument. Yet that in turn suggests another possibility, namely the ability of literature to catch the reader off guard, challenging assumptions or giving fresh understanding where we would not have looked for it.

To sum up, we are dealing with a two-way process. Setting out to read in the light of faith is one part of it. Finding that we ourselves are being 'read' by the texts we study, so that our preconceptions and certainties are laid out for fresh examination, is the other part. 'Reading faithfully' means being open to both parts of the process. Unavoidably, it means putting ourselves at risk.

An approach to faithful reading

This book sets out to introduce its readers to the two-way engagement with literature I have described. Its purpose is to help students who have already found that their literary experience leads them to reflect on matters of faith to gather skills for asking questions about the material they read, in the light of the Christian tradition. Many of the questions begin with ourselves, our situation in a particular set of circumstances, and our reactions to what we read. Here are some questions that may have arisen for you.

- Can literature show us Christ?
- Can literature represent our potential for both good and bad?
- What happens to our understanding of Scripture when it is rewritten in the form of poetry or drama?
- Are we permitted to talk about the failure of faith, our doubts, fears, despair or outright disbelief?
- Can adventurous ways of talking about God give new meaning to our experience of faith?
- Are there proper limits of religious language or language about the content of belief?
- Are there times when we should be shocked by literary treatments of matters of faith?

A very important part of this project has been choosing texts that allow such questions to be voiced and explored. The examples used here span a wide chronological range. The earliest text you will study is the Old Testament Book of *Ruth*. The most recent is a novel published in the 1990s. These examples are drawn from a correspondingly wide selection of genres: fiction, drama, poetry, biblical narrative and liturgical material. Not all of them have been written with a theological or devotional purpose.

All choices imply that other things have been excluded and this group is no exception. It is representative rather than definitive, and creates opportunities for students to address questions and make connections in ways that will equip them to read other texts enquiringly and perceptively. Students will be encouraged to:

- read a book of the Bible with careful attention to its operation as a work of literature;

- meet biblical narrative afresh in a re-telling by a much later writer;
- see the creative imagination at work in the composition of texts of prayer and praise;
- discover the adventurous possibilities for articulating our relationship with God inherent in language;
- see how various aspects of faith can be given a voice in literature – from despair and uncertainty to joyful conviction.

The practice of reading

Each chapter in this book asks you to read attentively, noticing ways of using language, arranging elements in a story, or plotting a theme that runs through a whole work. One of the intended outcomes is that students will emerge with a small initial critical vocabulary that will grow in the course of time. Critical terminology is not something to be learned for its own sake, but it can be a great advantage in describing the workings and effects of creative writing when it is properly used. Terms are introduced in context here, so that students can see how they are applied in practice.

Never assume when you are reading that a short work is an easy one. The exercise below will help you to understand why length is not a guide to complexity.

EXERCISE

📖 **Read this poem by George Herbert, 'Ana {MARY / ARMY} gram'.**

How well her name an Army doth present,
In whom the Lord of Hosts did pitch his tent!

Spend some time framing a summary of the poem and compare the length of your account with the two lines above.

Starting with the idea of the anagram – a word whose letters can be rearranged to spell another word – the couplet plays with the name of the Virgin Mary in order to show how apt it is in relation to God's purpose for her. There is much more to it than that, however. In two lines we have a tightly compressed statement of the mystery of the incarnation, in which God takes on human nature. 'The Lord of Hosts' is a frequent Old Testament title for God. It is also a military image referring to the leader of an army. Like a general setting up his camp on a battle-field, then, God makes a temporary dwelling on the human battlefield, and sojourns in the body of a mortal woman. All of these strands have been the subject of extensive theological discussion, and all of them have been celebrated in literature.

This tightly packed summary opens up a wealth of issues for further reflection in a deceptively simple manner. What could be more ordinary than pregnancy and birth? What could be more extraordinary than God becoming human, or God asking his own creation to co-operate in making that event possible? This joyful interplay between the everyday and the miraculous is a frequent theme in literature, and not only bib-lical and religious literature.

📖 **Read this sonnet by the contemporary poet, Gordon Jackson.**

It will help you to know that it comes from his collection *25 Domestic Sonnets* (1986). Although the poem has the flavour of autobiography, we do not have to read it as a scene from the poet's own life. We might assume, for dramatic purposes, that the poem is an address by the speaker to his wife. We might even read it as a wife speaking to her hus-band.

> The chairs you buy have all the marks of the fall
>   About them, torn fabric worn to threadbare,
> Springs deformed, stretched webbing, castors all
>   Askew or lost, the woodwork in despair.
>
> With love, and art, and elbow-grease, and time,
>   The broken-down looks up, the bent gains poise,
> The faint recovers strength, the crude grows fine,
>   The old renews, the humble poor rejoice.
>
> Salvation is much more than getting back
>   An ancient lustre lost, it is much more
> Than mere repair of what has gone to rack
>   And ruin: your work enriches what before
> Was merely good, redeems it from its lack
>   Of proper beauty, untransfigured law.

EXERCISE

Try to say what the poem is 'about'.

The first eight lines paint a vivid picture of activity over time. Can you explain how a particular process of change is made almost tangible for the reader by the descriptions in this passage?

What sort of change do you sense in the way the poem addresses you in the last six lines? Do you find this change of gear uncomfortable or illuminating?

You may have found it hard to decide at first whether you were reading a poem about furniture restoration, a love poem, or a poem describing something that encompasses both these possibilities in a much larger embrace. All of these represent levels or dimensions of the sonnet, and it takes the last six lines (or sestet) to help us make sense of what has gone before.

The initial picture brings to life the familiar occupation of home handiwork, and echoes the experience of all those people who take on the challenge of reupholstering and polishing old chairs to make them usable and attractive once again. There is more to it than this, however. For the restorer's art is not merely pragmatic, a necessary labour to make the domestic scene respectable. It is its own kind of love, expressed in patiently restoring dignity to objects that have been discarded by former owners who saw only their shabbiness and forgot that they had once been beautiful. The speaker, watching that loving dedication to the task of renewal, also learns again to love the renewer.

We leap from there to a metaphor of God's saving love for humankind, even though we never depart from the household reality the poem describes. What the mender and restorer of old chairs achieves is not just an item which is now as good as new. It is a new creation because it has been valued in a new way, and brought back to a state of beauty through the loving labour of someone who could see beneath its decrepit exterior to imagine what it might become. In the same way, God looks at the fallen creation, and patiently works with it, even becoming human, to bring it to the full measure of its potential.

How do we know that this is the connection the poem is asking us to make? At this point, the sense will emerge more richly if you are able to recognise echoes and allusions from worship and Scripture. If you look at lines 5 to 8, and compare them with the Magnificat, or Song of Mary, in the first chapter of St Luke's gospel (Luke 1:46–55), you will see a remarkable similarity. The version in *The Book of Common Prayer*'s order for Evening Prayer makes this especially clear. Mary rejoices with her cousin Elizabeth that the child she is carrying will be the liberation of Israel. He will not only restore their fortunes. He will also bring them to a transfigured relationship with God in a new bond or covenant.

This does not mean abolishing the old law, which held the People of Israel within a number of restrictive codes. Instead, it means fulfilling the law, and making God's promise of a saviour come true. Jesus himself makes this point (see Matthew 5:17). As St Paul tells the Corinthian Church, the written law on its own is sterile and condemns sinful human beings to death, but the Spirit of God, given under the new covenant, brings life – just such new life as might be seen in old chairs polished to a glorious shine (2 Corinthians 3:6).

You might have found this surprising and even a little irreverent. A little reflection, however, will help you to recall that God frequently appears to act unconventionally and in deliberate contravention of rules. The gospels tell of several healings that take place on the Sabbath against Jewish custom. Water turns into rather good wine at a wedding, perhaps for the sheer fun of prolonging the celebration and astonishing the guests. Much more darkly, Jesus presents his own body and blood symbolically at the Last Supper, and literally on the cross, as the food his followers must eat to carry them through the earthly journey to eternal life. Literature does not shirk the horror that this image implies.

📖 **Read these lines from the third part of Gordon Jackson's six-part poem on the Eucharist, *Charnal Supper* (1995).**

> ... and he is meat and drink for us and
> daily bread, even with jam on it,
> and manna that tastes like just what you
> want it to, cream cheese, caviare, veal,
> stuffed olives, oysters, lobster boiled in all the agony of cookery,
> he has borne all the griefs, the swollen
> goose's delicate liver, and the
> bleating lamb led to the slaughter that
> its mother witnesses, all of it
> he has borne under the baking sun,
> his back streaked by the tenderising

whips of professional lackeys, and
garnished with a mocking crown, basted
with his own blood, with vinegar to
quench his thirst he hangs accursed and blest
like all of us bearing our griefs and his
from the first fathering of time
until its last fulfilment . . .

EXERCISE

Describe your reaction to these lines. Think particularly hard about the aspects that you find confrontational or even revolting.

Try to say whether you think the poet has played fair with the reader, by introducing the vocabulary of the ordinary and pleasurable acts of cooking and eating into a reconstruction of the unbearable sight of Christ's passion.

If you felt that you could hardly stomach this extract, that was probably an appropriate reaction. There is no reason why we should feel comfortable with the crucifixion, or with any act of torture. But language grows tired with frequent use, and we become blunted to horrifying and inhumane events because we read about them every day in the newspapers and see them on television. They are always described in the same words: 'shocking', 'tragic', 'appalling', 'brutal'.

The lines you have read turn the conventions upside down by using ordinary language from a completely foreign activity (cookery) to convey the agony of Christ's suffering. He is tenderised, garnished and basted in the baking heat of Calvary.

There is a relentless logic in this. If Jesus' sacrificially given body is our food, why should it not be as carefully prepared as the Sunday roast or a banquet of exotic delicacies? If we are to believe that it is something tangible, everything we need for our salvation, then it must embrace every good thing we can think of (caviare and olives, for example) in its being. It must also be able to contain the suffering that goes into feeding us, whether it is the slaughter of a lamb or the forced fattening of a goose for the paté industry.

But what suggests this range of images? Much of it originates in the prophet Isaiah's depiction of the one who will suffer on behalf of all. He has 'borne our griefs' and 'carried our sorrows' (Isaiah 53:3, *Authorised Version*). He has been wounded and bruised and treated like a lamb led to the slaughter (Isaiah 53:5, 7). Only a slightly further stretch of the imagination takes the poet towards the ruthlessly meticulous process that begins with the fattening of an animal, and ends with its final decorative appearance on the festal dinner table.

It is that wholeness of vision, uncomfortable and unsettling though it may be, that distinguishes certain kinds of writing, and helps us to view the elements of our faith and worship with new insight.

Building on foundations

The exercises you have just attempted are a sample of what you will be asked to do at various points in the following chapters. Often, the purpose of an exercise is to draw attention to features of the writing that contribute to especially apt or striking ways of communicating with the reader. But the process does not end there. Good communication will always lead you further, towards a profounder sense of the work as a whole.

Do not forget, though, that the skills you learn from models of excellence are skills that can be taken into all your reading. Anyone who is tempted to draw early conclusions about works that are capable of leading to reflection on faith, and works that are not, should listen to the guidance of a critic who has worked extensively to develop the interdisciplinary enquiry of literature and theology (or literature and religion, as it is more commonly known in the United States). David Jasper begins his own introduction to the subject with T S Eliot's statement in his essay 'Religion and Literature' (first published in 1935) that he was 'not concerned . . . with religious literature, but with the application of our religion to the criticism of any literature'. Jasper points out that 'we may or may not agree with his judgements but at least we should recognize his endeavour to free the consideration of "literature and religion" from the limitations of devotional or even religious propagandist elements, however worthy these may be' (Jasper, 1992, p. 39).

Jasper sets out a way of achieving the kind of breadth that allows for open and constructive discussion of issues common to faith and literature. He emphasises the contribution of different theoretical approaches to addressing theological questions. Ethical issues, problems of faith and the complexities of divine justice are among the subjects that his book confronts through readings of literary examples.

This concern to keep the study of literature and theology on a large playing field is reflected in the range of recent publications, conference themes and courses taught in colleges and universities. Under this general subject heading, we are likely to encounter treatments of a wide variety of texts, by writers whose approaches to reading and criticism represent a diversity of interests and starting points. Increasingly, films, paintings and videos are entering discussions of the issues of faith raised by works of the creative imagination.

All of this testifies to a relationship with tradition that is fruitful and instructive. Literature and the creative arts return again and again to issues at the centre of human existence: love, the pursuit of happiness, hope, truth, and on the darker side evil, suffering and death. Biblical literature raises the issues in the light of faith in God's ultimately providential purpose for creation. Other works raise them differently. Sometimes, they ask for a theological response; sometimes they merely open the door to such a response, without explicitly or even consciously inviting it.

This book hopes to be a starting point for surprising, adventurous and above all honest exploration. Whatever knowledge or experience students bring will be an advantage, as long as it is understood that entering into a conversation with a text is a demanding business. The ability to apply the techniques that this study introduces will not by itself make us better readers. It can only commit us to engaging responsibly with what is before us, and at the same time, to pursuing a dialogue with what is behind us. In other words, we continue to inhabit a conversation between the novels, poems and plays we read, and the biblical, literary and liturgical traditions that have shaped both texts and their readers.

Further reading

Brown, D and Fuller, D (1995), *Signs of Grace: sacraments in poetry and prose*, London, Cassell.

Brown, D and Loades, A (1996), *Christ the Sacramental Word*, London, SPCK.

Drabble, M and Stringer, J (eds) (1985), *The Oxford Companion to English Literature*, Oxford, Oxford University Press (fifth edition).

Edwards, M (1984), *Towards a Christian Poetics*, London, Macmillan.

Eliot, T S (1951), Religion and Literature, in *Selected Essays*, pp. 388–401, London, Faber and Faber (third edition).

Evans, R (1999), *Using the Bible: studying the text*, London, Darton, Longman and Todd.

Gearon, L (ed.) (1999), *English Literature, Theology and the Curriculum*, London, Cassell.

Jasper, D (1992), *The Study of Literature and Religion: an introduction*, Basingstoke, Macmillan (second edition).

Lodge, D (1999), *Modern Criticism and Theory: a reader*, London, Longman (second edition).

Wright, T (1988), *Theology and Literature*, Oxford, Blackwell.

Wynne-Davies, M (ed.) (1997), *The Bloomsbury Dictionary of English Literature*, London, Bloomsbury.

2. TELLING GOD'S STORY

Introduction

This chapter concentrates on a single biblical narrative – the Old Testament story of Ruth – as a way of exploring a literary approach to the Bible. Robert Alter, whose book *The Art of Biblical Narrative* is an important resource, has written scathingly of a trend towards discussing the Bible as literature. The Bible, he argues, is self-evidently literature in a variety of sophisticated genres. What its readers need to discover is a way of paying attention to its techniques of relating history, or telling a story for the purpose of instruction. This means bringing to bear on the biblical text the same expectations of artistry and skill that we might apply to any other work, though with the expectation that the more clearly we grasp the workings of the text, the more acutely we will understand that every device counts in the communication of a message or story. Reading *Ruth* is a splendid way to meet a text that is both a story in literary terms and an episode with important consequences in the larger scheme of biblical history.

    📖 **Read *Ruth* several times.** If possible, read it in more than one modern translation (for example *The New Revised Standard Version* and *The Revised English Bible*). You might also compare a modern paraphrase such as *The Good News Bible*. Different translations give different nuances to biblical stories, even though the details might be identical.

    Ruth is, in one sense, a self-contained short story. With extraordinary economy, it tells of a family's departure from the land God had given his people, their foreign marriages, the misfortunes they suffer through illness and death, and the restoration of their happiness and prosperity when two of the survivors return to Bethlehem. From that point of view, the narrative could stand alone. It is perfectly capable of being understood without reference to other biblical episodes.

In another sense, the narrator has deliberately forged links that remind us how Ruth's history meshes with the greater history of God's relationship with his people. As our discussion progresses, we will be looking at its pointers to a place in biblical chronology, and at the associations it suggests with other biblical characters. At that stage, we will introduce matters of law and custom that govern the events of the tale. It will be appropriate to ask how Ruth, Naomi and Boaz perceive themselves. Are they conscious of their key role in the later history of a people?

Reflecting on experience

Have you ever been in a situation where you felt foreign or alien? This may have been in a literal sense (perhaps while staying in another country) or in a metaphorical sense (for example in circumstances which you did not understand and where you had no connection with other people present).

Try to recall any associated feelings, such as fear, confusion or loneliness.

Have you ever had to make a decision about your loyalty to a particular person, knowing that your own security might be threatened by pursuing your care and responsibility for the other person?

Ruth as a short story

As I suggested at the outset, there are various ways of approaching the story of Ruth. We will begin by treating it as a short story, independent of any larger context. There are particular reasons for this choice. A reading of this kind devotes all its attention to the events that occur within the frame of the narrative. It applies the techniques we would use to approach any work of fiction, and looks for ways to make sense of the work as a whole in the characters' relationships with each other, in the pattern of their experiences and in symbolic features such as meaningful names or (as in this case) contrasting images of barrenness and despair, fertility and hope. This is not sufficient in itself as a reading of a biblical text, but it is a valuable exercise in conjunction with other tools of interpretation.

The tale begins with a broad survey of the history of a family. Elimelech and his wife Naomi leave Judah with their two sons, Mahlon and Chilion, for the neighbouring country of Moab. There is no reason for this move, and we are told only of what happened subsequently. Elimelech dies, and his sons marry the Moabite women, Orpah and Ruth. About ten years pass and the sons die too. This leaves Naomi with a decision to make about her future and she chooses to return to her own country. Ruth and Orpah are initially equally determined to follow. In the end, though, it is only Ruth who persists in this course, making a firm declaration of loyalty to her mother-in-law. The two women find their way back to Bethlehem, where Naomi is recognised and greeted by name. Her reply asks that her name be changed to Mara, meaning bitter, because the Lord has dealt with her bitterly.

EXERCISE

This is an opportunity to think about the names of the other characters. Elimelech means 'my God is king'; Mahlon and Chilion mean 'weakening and pining' or 'blot out and perish'; Naomi means 'winsome' or 'my lovely one'; Orpah means 'the nape of the neck' (a back view, significantly); Ruth is related to a word meaning 'soaked or well-watered' (though it is sometimes mistranslated 'friendship'). What relationship do you see between these names and the family's experiences of prosperity and hardship?

The next scene takes us to the barley field where Ruth has gone to glean, hoping that she will benefit from the kindness of the owner of the land. At this point, we are dependent on a brief but significant detail: the episode opens with a reference to Naomi's relative, Boaz, who belongs to the family of Elimelech. It is Boaz's field that Ruth chooses to glean in, although it is clear that she is unaware of any tie of kinship. The audience might thus anticipate, in a tale where no words are wasted, that there will be important consequences.

Even before he has spoken to Ruth, Boaz appears to have singled her out. On the one hand, this may be no more than the action of a responsible farmer who cannot afford to have strangers on his land at harvest-time. On the other hand, it does suggest a framework or context for what is to happen later.

EXERCISE
📖 **Re-read Ruth 2:8–13.**

Think carefully about Boaz's motives for treating Ruth protectively and the actions for which he admires her. Your conclusions will be important when we come to the next phase of the narrative.

By the end of the first day's work, Ruth has been fed and given more barley than she could have gleaned had she not had special privileges (2:16). When her daughter-in-law returns with forty litres (or twenty kilograms or about 45 pounds) of grain, Naomi is delighted that a local landowner could have been so generous. She is even more delighted when she learns that the benefactor is Boaz. At this point, the two women's thoughts seem to be directed towards different interests. Naomi exclaims, 'Blessings on him from the Lord, who has kept faith with the living and the dead!' (2:20), perhaps thinking already about settling Ruth in the security of a second marriage. Ruth, however, is still recollecting the events of the day and in particular Boaz's instruction to her to stay close to his labourers until the harvest is over. This points to an interest in Boaz the individual, rather than Boaz the potential redeemer of the family fortunes. So another scene ends.

The beginning of the third chapter of *Ruth* reveals that Naomi's mind has been active during the harvest season. Now it is the end of that time, when the barley has been gathered for threshing, and the two women have their future to consider. Naomi explains a rather daring plan to Ruth, which involves elaborate preparations for a nocturnal visit to the threshing floor, where Boaz will be spending the night.

EXERCISE
Modern English translations of *Ruth* record Naomi's instructions (3:1–5) and conclude with her prediction that Boaz will tell Ruth 'what to do'. This is the case in *The Revised English Bible, The New Revised Standard Version* and *The New Jerusalem Bible. The Living Bible*, which is a paraphrase rather than a translation,   ▶▶

is much more explicit about the fact that marriage is the intended outcome of this plan. Boaz, Naomi says in this version, will tell Ruth 'what to do about marriage'.

These examples show the differences between a subtle technique that works by means of hints and suggestions, and an overt statement. What effect do these different versions have on your response to the way the story develops?

At this juncture, we need to weigh the narrative presentation of the characters' motivation against what might seem a more plausible account of their actions. Are Ruth and Boaz really little more than passive figures in a scheme orchestrated entirely by Naomi? Surely Ruth's action demonstrates a high degree of initiative, and a certain risk-taking temperament that will break the conventions governing the approaches that women may make to men? As Mieke Bal points out, in a book called *Lethal Love* that explores a number of biblical love stories from a feminist perspective, the Hebrew word for 'feet' (3:4) is ambiguous, and is also capable of being interpreted as 'genitals'. Such a reading underlines Ruth's assertiveness and suggests that Boaz, once he had recovered from the surprise of finding her beside him, was quite ready to pursue the sexual invitation. Ruth's departure 'before it was light enough for one man to recognise another' (*Revised English Bible*) tends to support this impression.

EXERCISE
Mieke Bal draws attention to Boaz's praise for Ruth's second great kindness at this moment, because she has not gone after young men. You will remember that the first time he remarks on her kindness (2:11) he is referring to her care for Naomi. Bal suggests that we might see in this an older man's gratitude for a younger woman's attention (Bal, 1987, pp. 83–84). Notice that it is a little later that he mentions Naomi: it is unlikely that he was thinking of her when he commended Ruth.

Reflect on the relationship between Ruth and Boaz in the light of this proposal. Does Bal's interpretation persuade you?

The final scene of *Ruth* records the legal negotiations for the right to marry a widowed kinswoman that must precede Ruth's marriage to Boaz. Here, it is apparent that Boaz has planned a careful strategy. He approaches the member of the family with prior rights with only partial information, relating to the security of land owned by Naomi's husband Elimelech. Once he has gained the man's agreement to act as the redeemer of this land, he reveals that Ruth is part of the bargain. As the next section of the chapter shows, this has implications for ownership rights that deter the man from taking on the role Boaz has suggested. Anyone who married Ruth would eventually have to cede her land to the sons born of the marriage, who would legally be the heirs of Ruth's dead husband. The path is thus clear for Boaz to marry Ruth.

A happy ending follows. In due course, Ruth has a son, to the great joy of Naomi who becomes an adoptive grandmother. Placing the child in her lap follows an adoption ritual found elsewhere in ancient Near Eastern culture. There are certain anomalies about this last gesture. We would expect the parents of a newborn child to name him. The intervention of friends of someone who is not even his grandmother by blood seems a strange feature of the tale. To attempt an explanation, we need to return to *Ruth*, this time viewing the book as an episode in biblical history.

Ruth as history

The reading we have just concluded deliberately avoids addressing a number of narrative details. Nothing has yet been said about indications of *Ruth's* place in the chronology of God's people, or about the significance of its geographical setting. Equally, we have not tried to understand Naomi's bitter joke (1:11–13), the terms on which Ruth is allowed to glean in Boaz's fields, and the law that has to be negotiated before Boaz may marry Ruth.

'Once, in the time of the Judges' (the words that begin *The Revised English Bible*'s account) is not at all the same thing as the conventional folktale opening, 'Once upon a time'. The story of Ruth is related to real events, and to a time, as Jack Sasson has noted in an illuminating essay on the book, when 'people were constantly losing God's grace before earning it again' (1989, p. 322). Elimelech and Naomi's move to Moab, the land populated by the descendants of Lot's incestuous relationship with his daughter (Genesis 19:30–38) and their sons' foreign marriages, may not have pleased God. The fate of the family, as you have already noticed, is written particularly poignantly into the meaning of the sons' names. Again, Sasson calls attention to the fact that 'symbolic names of this sort are not typical of Hebrew narrative and may once more betray an edifying purpose in *Ruth*' (1989, p. 322).

The decision that follows the deaths of all the men in the first chapter of the story opens up two issues of custom. First of all, the expectation after such events would be that the young widows, Ruth and Orpah, would return to their former parental homes in Moab. There is no tie, apart from the tie of affection, binding them to Naomi, nor do they have any children who might be regarded as the responsibility of the extended family in Judah. The second matter is the custom of so-called *levirate* marriage.

EXERCISE
📖 Read Naomi's words in Ruth 1:12–13 and then read Deuteronomy 25:5–10.

The second passage explains the process of levirate marriage. In the light of the comparison, try to state the thinking that lies behind Naomi's words.

In reading Naomi's exhortation to her daughters-in-law alongside a relevant passage in the Law, you will probably have concluded that all the characters recognise the impossibility of a levirate marriage. The older woman evidently feels it better that Orpah and Ruth should attempt to marry again within their own people. She is in no way urging them to return with her to Bethlehem to demand their right to perpetuate their husbands' names under the law of the levirate. Ruth's personal loyalty to Naomi is to be seen in the force of her oath (1:16–17). It follows the formula of a vow followed by a strong hint at the curses that will fall on the one who fails to keep the vow – although it was considered unlucky to name the likely misfortunes specifically.

So it is that Ruth and Naomi find themselves in Bethlehem, and faced with the problem of supporting themselves. The Law allowed the poor and the alien to glean after the harvesters had gathered in the crop (see Leviticus 19:9–10; 23:22 and Deuteronomy 24:19–22). But the implementing of the Law depended a great deal on the kindness of individual landowners. That Boaz is both generous and a kinsman seems almost too good to be true.

EXERCISE

Naomi announces happily that Boaz is a relation (2:20). The significance of her remark in the Hebrew is sharper than this. She identifies Boaz as 'one of our *go'elim*'. The *go'el* had a duty to prevent land belonging to a family from falling into other hands after a death (see Leviticus 25:23–25).

Consider what this role might imply for the decision that has to be made later (4:1–5). Why does Boaz have to present Ruth's case in the way he does?

The plan that evolves comes about in part, perhaps, because Naomi sees that Boaz is personally well-disposed to Ruth, and therefore likely to be willing to offer his protection as a kinsman. There is some evidence to suggest that Ruth's request that he spread his cloak over her is an outright proposal of marriage, or at least a request to be taken into his household, for the metaphor of spreading out a cloak has that meaning elsewhere (Deuteronomy 23:1 and Ezekiel 16). But there is an obstacle: Boaz is not in fact the nearest blood-relative. To marry Ruth and redeem her land all at once, he must first persuade the nearer kinsman to renounce his claim.

What follows suggests a certain measure of duplicity. Having gained this man's agreement to redeem the land, Boaz announces that his plan is to take over Ruth to continue Mahlon's name on the property (4:5). Jack Sasson argues that the future tense of taking over or acquiring is a mistranslation that has persisted over many centuries. In fact, he says, Boaz speaks of something that has already happened. Whether or not the closer relation redeems the land, it is Boaz's intention to father a child by Ruth. Although the land belongs to Naomi, and the kinsman's primary duty is to her, any child of Ruth and Boaz will automatically become the heir. There is thus no advantage for the other man in this arrangement, and the way is clear for Boaz. Ruth's son Obed, adopted by Naomi and named by local women, becomes not only the continuation of one family but also the father of the more illustrious family that will produce King David (Sasson, 1989, pp. 326–327).

A place in the tradition

Read through a historical lens, *Ruth* takes up a place in the covenantal relationship between God and his people. The story itself shows considerable awareness of other stories whose particular details help to interpret this one. Jacob's twelve sons by Rachel and Leah become the fathers of the twelve tribes of Israel. Perez, the son of Tamar and Judah, also stands in the Davidic line. Yet this is really a story about mothers rather than fathers.

EXERCISE
📖 **Read Genesis 29, 30 and 38.**

Take careful note of the circumstances in which marriages or relationships are contracted in both cases, especially where aspects of the account seem unusual. Also, be attentive to the initiative shown by various characters.

Your reading will have confirmed that there are distinctly unconventional aspects in both narratives. Jacob is deceived by his father-in-law, Laban, into marrying both his daughters. Having had Leah, whom he does not love, forced upon him, he is made to work for a further seven years for Rachel, whom he does love. Leah gives birth to a number of children; Rachel is childless for many years. Eventually, the sisters collude in Jacob's escape from Laban's control, even going so far as to steal their father's household gods. Mieke Bal suggests that the writer of *Ruth* employs a doubling technique in naming both Rachel and Leah. Together, the sisters combine love and fertility. In Ruth, both elements are combined (Bal, 1987, pp. 84–85).

Tamar's history is even more remarkable. Deprived by her father-in-law, Judah, of the right to a child fathered by one of her deceased husband's brothers, she lures him into fathering her twin sons himself by posing as a temple prostitute. When she produces tokens to prove this just before he is about to have her executed, he is obliged to admit that she was more in the right than he was.

The point on both occasions is that the success of the family is achieved by trickery and transgression, mainly on the part of the female protagonists.

📖 **Read the following passage.** It is a very strong reading of the place of Ruth alongside Leah, Rachel and Tamar. Allow time to think about it, and if you have the opportunity, discuss it with other students.

> The series of transgressing women tells a story by analogy, dispersed among several episodes, but still coherent: 'the continuity of history, or how to admit love.' In other words: the building of the house of Israel, against all odds, against fearful fathers. (Bal, 1987, p. 131)

Naomi and Ruth fit very comfortably into this pattern, however we finally choose to see their individual roles in achieving the marriage of Ruth and Boaz. Between them, they have redeemed their land and produced an heir. Ruth, a foreign woman, has not only found a secure place amongst her mother-in-law's people, she has also taken a prominent role in the ancestry of that nation's greatest king.

In this light, the final genealogy that stretches from Perez to David does little justice to the extraordinary determination of these women. It traces the line of descent through Boaz, and completely omits the name of Elimelech, whose memory is at stake in the story. The notes to *The New Jerusalem Bible* stress that the second genealogy 'cannot be the work of the author of Ruth'. It must be supposed to be a later addition, written with the purpose of revealing a different continuity between the line of Abraham, Isaac and Jacob, and David. God's promise, in other words, has remained steadfast across all those generations. But the price to be paid for that demonstration of the covenant is the eclipse of the story's most engaging characters.

Whose story?

The constant feature, whether we end the tale at 4:17 or continue through 4:18–22, is the presence of David at the end of the family history. A small group's adventures prove to have far-reaching consequences. Do the characters themselves foresee the potential long-term effects of their actions? Gabriel Josipovici is one commentator who has asked that question. In a reflection on Tamar's deception of Judah and the dynastic implications of her action (Genesis 38:13–14), he argues that she 'does what she does not because she knows she is part of the story, but because she feels in an obscure way that she has to do what is right: beget children, and beget them from the family of Judah. She no more knows that her line will be that of David than does Ruth when she lies beside Boaz' (Josipovici, 1988, p. 289).

Like Tamar, Ruth and Naomi act in ways that fulfil the conditions of the law of kinship. Nor is it ever quite clear who is the central figure. The book is named for Ruth, yet in the end it is Naomi who retrieves her land and sees her husband's name continued through the child of his kinsman Boaz, and Ruth. As we have seen, it was left to a later hand to add the genealogy that confirms their children's place in a history greater than they could have imagined. An appropriate response must take account of both the smaller and the larger view. The Christian tradition sees the Old Testament fulfilled in the New Testament, and celebrates the connection of the incarnate Jesus to the house of David. Within that overarching story are other cameos, like Ruth, whose lives and adventures reconfirm the promise while drawing characters with more than a simply two-dimensional existence.

Further reading

Barton, J (1998), Historical-critical approaches, in J Barton (ed.), *The Cambridge Companion to Biblical Interpretation*, pp. 9–20, Cambridge, Cambridge University Press.

Brown, R E, Fitzmyer, J A and Murphy, R E (eds) (1990), *The New Jerome Biblical Commentary*, London, Chapman.

Darr, K P (1991), 'More than Seven Sons': critical, rabbinical and feminist perspectives on Ruth, in *Far More Precious than Jewels: perspectives on biblical women*, pp. 55–84, Louisville, Kentucky, Westminster/John Knox Press.

Exum, J C (1996), Is this Naomi?, in *Plotted, Shot and Painted: cultural representations of biblical women*, pp. 129–174, Sheffield, Sheffield Academic Press.

Jasper, D (1998), Literary readings of the Bible, in J Barton (ed.), *The Cambridge Companion to Biblical Interpretation*, pp. 21–34, Cambridge, Cambridge University Press.

Schwartz, R (ed.) (1990), *The Book and the Text: the Bible and literary theory*, Oxford, Blackwell.

3. PRAYER AND PRAISE

Introduction

In this chapter, we discuss the language of liturgy or worship, as both communication with God in prayer and praise, and literary creation. 'Liturgy' comes from a Greek word that referred originally to a form of public service or benefaction. It might, for example, have described a procession or presentation funded by a successful general returning from a military campaign. Later, it took on the more restricted meaning of service given to God, in the shape of formal acts of prayer and praise.

Reflecting on experience

Contemporary experiences of liturgy differ widely. For some people, regular attendance at a local church would be a normal pattern. Others might choose to visit churches or house-groups of various traditions rather than to commit themselves to a single worshipping community. Still others may only ever encounter religion in the form of weddings, funerals and baptisms.

How would you describe your own experience of liturgy?

Across the Christian tradition, *liturgy* may be used to suggest various activities under the general heading of worship. For the Orthodox Churches of the Eastern tradition, it refers specifically to the celebration of the Eucharist. It may be used in a phrase like 'Anglican liturgy' to indicate all the services that form part of the Anglican tradition of worship. It may be used to describe rites alone, or it may include the music used in worship. The rites that contemporary Christianity inherits from the early Church (mainly eucharistic rites) are often known by the name of the Church Fathers with whom they were associated, for example the

Liturgy of Saint Basil and the Liturgy of Saint John Chrysostom. Among modern patterns of worship, we are now accustomed to hearing of, and sometimes using, the Taizé Liturgy developed by the Taizé Community in France, and the Iona Liturgy that comes from the community living and working on the Scottish island of Iona.

Liturgy is a vast subject, and for that reason the scope of this chapter is conservative. The three texts to be examined are all in English and come from the liturgical repertoire of mainstream Christian denominations. Within those boundaries, we will try to say something about the characteristics of liturgical composition. Among these it is worth drawing attention immediately to scriptural reference, the use of a range of images for God and for the relationship between human beings and God, and the importance of repetition in establishing the rhythm of prayer.

Fixed forms of prayer can be 'owned' by a community of worshippers and perhaps even provide a focus of identity across a very wide geographical area. The prime example of this is the Latin Mass, which was the standard form for Roman Catholics across the globe until relatively recently. Related to this, an inherited tradition of worship helps to link its users to those who have followed the path of faith before them. But we should never forget that prayer always has its roots in a particular culture. The final text to be considered shows how material can be adapted for use by worshippers from a different cultural background. In other words, good liturgical writing allows tradition and diversity to live together in harmony.

It is difficult to suggest appropriate preparatory reading without seeming arbitrary. Students from traditions where prescribed forms of worship are the norm should start by familiarising themselves with the contents of the prayer book or collection of services used in their place of worship. Attentive and questioning participation will lay excellent foundations for further study. Students accustomed to informal worship should not be intimidated. The suggestions for further reading will help to explain the concepts to be introduced here.

EXERCISE

Make a list of the prayers that are most familiar to you, or of some favourite prayers from your own experience of worship. Then make a list of your favourite short poems. What similarities ▶▶

> in style, rhythm, and use of pictorial language exist between the two lists? Would you be able to say why the prayers are not poems, or why the poems (even if they address religious themes) are not prayers?

The making of prayer

The prayer that follows first appeared in the earliest version of what came to be known as *The Book of Common Prayer*. It is still recited in Anglican churches on the first Sunday of Advent.

📖 **Read the collect for the First Sunday in Advent (*Book of Common Prayer*), preferably aloud.** If you are uncertain about the place of Advent in the seasons of the Church's year, or about the use of collects, look up the relevant entries in a dictionary of liturgy or in a dictionary of the Church. References are given at the end of the chapter.

> Almighty God, give us grace that we may cast away the works of darkness, and put upon us the armour of light, now in the time of this mortal life, in which thy Son Jesus Christ came to visit us in great humility; that in the last day, when he shall come again in his glorious majesty to judge both the quick and the dead, we may rise to the life immortal, through him who liveth and reigneth with thee and the Holy Ghost, now and ever. Amen.

Traditionally, Advent is a time for eschatological reflection. (The Greek word *eschaton* means the end.) In other words, it concentrates on the end of earthly existence, and the promises of salvation and eternal life. The collect is a petition for God's assistance in making Christians ready to meet Christ at the second coming, as they prepare to celebrate his first coming at Christmas.

The composition of the prayer relies on a range of literary techniques to convey a message that unfolds dramatically under close examination. You may have observed that it works largely by setting up oppositions or antitheses. Thus 'the works of darkness' are set against 'the armour of light'; 'this mortal life' against 'the life immortal'; 'humility' against 'majesty'. Simple though these polarities may seem, they mark some of the great distinctions of the Christian life. The constant struggle against the darkness of evil can only be waged in the faith that all evil is ultimately penetrated by the light of Christ. Human life, with its obvious physical ending, looks always for the transformation that is promised through Christ's resurrection (see, for example, the classic statement in 1 Corinthians 15). And all of this is understood against the astonishing fact that God took human shape in humility, in order to raise human nature to the majesty of his presence. These claims are made with considerable sophistication.

The prayer operates between 'now' and 'the last day'. The contrast between 'mortal life' and 'the life immortal' reveals itself not only at the level of sense, but also in the inversion of adjective and noun in 'the life immortal'. Finally, the mystery of Christ's entry into human life finds expression in the apparently self-contradictory term 'great humility'. In a straightforward way, this is a measure of quantity, of how humble God incarnate really is. But the figure is also an oxymoron – a nonsensical pair in which the first part seems to be radically opposed to the second. It requires that we ask what divine greatness has to do with human nature, and that question in turn opens up an enquiry into the working of God's grace.

Picturing belief

There is still more to say. Theological concepts are often expressed in metaphors. In this way, they become somehow concrete and accessible to the understanding of a wide range of people. At the same time, they make an impact on the imagination that enables statements of doctrine or belief to become part of a narrative or dramatic sense of the journey of faith.

EXERCISE

Discuss the examples of metaphor in the following extract from the collect:

> give us grace to cast away the works of darkness, and put upon us the armour of light.

Where have you encountered these images before?

How helpful do you find it to use pictorial language in order to articulate the struggle to reject evil and follow the Christian path?

Light and darkness are conventional metaphors for good and evil. Here, they are elaborated to suggest a military struggle. The actions of an evil life can only be combated by a determined campaign, and for this the Christian soldier (another popular and widely used image) must be properly equipped. Standard weaponry is, of course, no good in this cosmic battle. Only the light of Christ will defend the person under attack from temptation and sin. So a determined decision has to be made to reject all things that oppose the way of goodness, and to adopt the clothing of a new way of life. This should remind you of the symbolism of Christian baptism, which also uses reclothing to show that the newly baptised person has put Christ on like a garment.

What is the source of these images? To answer this question, it is important to know something about the context of the collect. First used in 1549, when it appeared in the First Book of Common Prayer published in the reign of Edward VI, it accompanied a reading from St Paul's Letter to the Romans (Romans 13:8–14). Verses 11 to 14 dwell on the need to wake up out of sleep and to get ready for the coming of Christ. The collect's metaphor of armed struggle against evil comes directly from this passage.

This illustrates a characteristic of much formal prayer: it is frequently inspired by biblical texts. The relationship is a dynamic one, interpreting the text in a new light that is relevant to a specific occasion or set of needs, and also giving to those who use the prayer a connection (conscious or otherwise) with a tradition of prayer and instruction.

Worship in song

The collect you have just studied stands firmly in the tradition of Anglican public worship, especially as it developed from the first official English language prayer book. Hymn-singing, which we now take for granted in most congregational acts of worship, was not quite such an early development. The Church was accustomed to psalms and canticles, but other forms of singing were not encouraged. It was in the eighteenth century, and particularly through the efforts of the Wesley brothers who were leaders of the Methodist movement (not then separate from the Church of England), that hymns became a familiar way of praising God.

Hymns provide the opportunity for a reflection on Scripture and belief that is quite different from formal prayer. David Jasper describes them in this way:

Hymns are verses with a specific task to do. They have to be sung, and to be immediately comprehensible to a congregation. They are an adjunct to worship and not solitary reflections upon religious experience. They are concerned with Christianity in its public form, as doctrine. At best, therefore, they are vehicles for a fine, sharp intellectualism, using compressed and clear language to express the concrete and particular matter of Christian belief. (Jasper, 1992, pp. 23–24)

The following hymn by Isaac Watts (1674–1748), a nonconformist hymn-writer, is a powerful meditation on the personal meaning of the cross for the individual believer:

When I survey the wondrous Cross
  On which the Prince of Glory died,
My richest gain I count but loss,
  And pour contempt on all my pride.

Forbid it, Lord, that I should boast
  Save in the death of Christ, my God;
All the vain things that charm me most,
  I sacrifice them to his blood.

See from his head, his hands, his feet,
  Sorrow and love flow mingled down;
Did e'er such love and sorrow meet?
  Or thorns compose so rich a crown?

His dying crimson like a robe,
  Spreads o'er his body on the Tree,
Then am I dead to all the globe,
  And all the globe is dead to me.

Were the whole realm of nature mine,
  That were a present far too small;
Love so amazing, so divine,
  Demands my soul, my life, my all.

EXERCISE
Imagine yourself in the situation the speaker describes. What sort of departure does this picture make from conventional ways of approaching the crucifixion of Jesus?

Reflect carefully on any particular elements of the description that strike you as startling or shocking, and try to say whether they are useful or obstructive to your own thinking about the meaning of the crucifixion.

Perhaps the most extraordinary aspect of this hymn is its manipulation of language to suggest an eye-witness account of the crucifixion. We are not certain, at first, whether the speaker is allowing his imagination to be led from a cross seen possibly in a church, backwards in time to the events on Calvary. Later on, it seems that the description comes directly and vividly from the foot of the cross itself.

The first two verses set down the guidelines for the speaker's meditation. Just as prayers are often informed by close reference to biblical texts, so here the epistles of Paul have provided a way of looking at the world in the light of the knowledge that Christ died to save the world.

EXERCISE
📖 Read Philippians 3:7–9 and Galatians 6:14. If possible use both the Authorised (King James) Version and a modern translation.

Watts would have been familiar with the King James Bible and this will have influenced the choice of certain words. Make notes of correspondences between the first two verses and these biblical references.

Paul understands the crucifixion as an event that overturns worldly systems of values. The cross alone endows the world it saves with value. Without it, nothing else has any importance or meaning.

Verses 3 to 5 return, imaginatively, to the scene of the crucifixion to paint a mesmeric and almost animated picture of the dying Christ. The bleeding body dominates the description. Blood seeps from every wound – head, hands, feet and finally side – until it flows together into one garment-like mass and envelops the man on the cross. How does the image escape sentimentality on the one hand and the grotesque on the other? To answer that question, we need to reflect on Christ's blood as the symbol of the life he gave to redeem humanity. It is a gift with a double motivation rooted in sorrow for the world's sins, and a love for the human creation too deep to allow sinful human beings to be lost. The 'sorrow and love' that the speaker reads into the streaks of blood on Jesus' face are far removed from sugary piety, while the 'dying crimson' has all the dignity of a royal robe. The cross is the triumph of a dying king whose death is solemn, dignified and awe-inspiring under conditions of the greatest humiliation. This is a central Christian paradox, or impossible possibility. Logically, kingship is not shown best in humiliation. In Christ's case, the crucifixion is the evidence of victory.

Verse 4 pursues the paradox of the cross by suggesting that it is not Christ, but the speaker, who dies when witnessing the very act of salvation. It takes us back to Galatians 6:14 with its world-changing interpretation of the cross as the one thing that entitles Christians to boast.

All of this is leading to a radical and complete commitment from the speaker. Having seen God die, he realises that he has nothing to give in return that could in any way reciprocate that gift. It demands the dedication of the whole person.

EXERCISE

Consider whether you would agree that this hymn is an exposition or teasing out of the meaning of Paul's teaching about the cross.

Do you find it helpful to approach the mystery of salvation in pictures?

Could you define the hymn as prayer, meditation or teaching, or would you choose another term or a combination of these labels?

Worship and culture

Our final example introduces a way of adapting traditional texts of worship for the needs of a particular worshipping community. The

Benedicite Aotearoa comes from the Anglican Province of New Zealand. It recasts the traditional song of thanksgiving, called the *Benedicite* from the first word of the Latin text, to make the words an act of praise with direct significance for a community encompassing Christians with very different histories: Maori, descendants of European settlers, and more recent immigrants.

📖 **Read the Benedicite Aotearoa:**

1. O give thanks to our God who is good:
   whose love endures for ever.

2. You sun and moon, you stars of the southern sky:
   give to our God your thanks and praise.

3. Sunrise and sunset, night and day:
   give to our God your thanks and praise.

4. All mountains and valleys, grassland and scree,
      glacier, avalanche, mist and snow:
   give to our God your thanks and praise.

5. You kauri and pine, rata and kowhai, mosses and ferns:
   give to our God your thanks and praise.

6. Dolphins and kahawai, sealion and crab,
      coral, anemone, pipi and shrimp:
   give to our God your thanks and praise.

7. Rabbits and cattle, moths and dogs,
      kiwi and sparrow and tui and hawk:
   give to our God your thanks and praise.

8. You Maori and Pakeha, women and men,
      all who inhabit the long white cloud:
   give to our God your thanks and praise.

9. All you saints and martyrs of the South Pacific:
   give to our God your thanks and praise.

10. All prophets and priests, all cleaners and clerks,
       professors, shop workers, typists and teachers,

job-seekers, invalids, drivers and doctors:
give to our God your thanks and praise.

11. All sweepers and diplomats, writers and artists,
grocers, carpenters, students and stock-agents,
seafarers, farmers, bakers and mystics:
give to our God your thanks and praise.

12. All children and infants, all people who play:
give to our God your thanks and praise.

This song of praise, in the shape it has here, represents the determination of those responsible for producing official forms of worship to include the double heritage of New Zealand: its indigenous Maori people whose name for it is Aotearoa (Land of the Long White Cloud), and the descendants of the white settlers (Pakeha in the Maori language) who came much later. But it has its roots elsewhere. The text is based on verses from the deuterocanonical or apocryphal chapters from the Greek version of the Old Testament Book of Daniel, in which the three young men who have been consigned to the furnace by Nebuchadnezzar sing a song of praise to God. It has been used by the Church as a canticle, or short biblical song, for a very long time. In the versions found in *The Book of Common Prayer* and modern language prayer books, the biblical verses are quoted without significant alteration. The purpose of studying the version from Aotearoa-New Zealand is to discover how a different set of cultural needs can influence change and development in forms of prayer and praise.

EXERCISE

📖 Read the 'Song of the Three' ('The Prayer of Azariah and the Song of the Three'). You will find this in a version of the Bible that includes the Apocrypha.

If you are able to do so, compare the version included in *The Book of Common Prayer* Order for Morning Prayer. Then carefully re-read *Benedicite Aotearoa*. What similarities and differences seem most noticeable?

The essence of all the versions of the biblical verses you have compared is the whole creation's offering of praise to God. At the same time, it is immediately clear that *Benedicite Aotearoa* is usable only in the local context of worship. Its references are deliberately specific where the original models employ more general categories. Thus the 'stars of the *southern* sky' are named, as are features of the New Zealand landscape and creatures native to the region. The people appear with their Maori names (verse 8) and the country itself has its evocative Maori name, translated as 'the land of the long white cloud'.

Where the models for the song distinguish categories of people broadly as 'priests' and 'servants', our example rejoices in a seemingly random and non-hierarchical assortment of occupations and callings. This list with no order to it brings together all human beings for the primary purpose of praising God. Status, qualifications and experience are unimportant beside the ability to belong to a community defined by its common wish to worship its creator. To reinforce that statement, the song calls on the devices of poetic language to set up new and perhaps unlikely relationships. Chiefly by means of a loose pattern of alliteration, occupations with an obvious bond, and those with little in common come together. The following lines use bold type to show how the sound-associations are made:

> All **p**rophets and **p**riests, all **c**leaners and **c**lerks,
> **p**rofessors, **sh**op workers, **t**ypists and **t**eachers

Holding all together, though, is the rhythmical repetition of the refrain, 'give to our God your thanks and praise'. This is a universal demand, reminding worshippers that all creation is God-given, and that all diversity issues from a common centre.

EXERCISE

Discuss the relationship between those elements of *Benedicite Aotearoa* that are particular to New Zealand and those that involve the whole of creation.

How do the two streams (local and universal) express the connection between believers in one place and believers worldwide?

Final reflection

The three texts for worship that this chapter has introduced have called overtly on what readers bring from both their literary and their theological experience. While they can be studied in a way that shows how they work poetically, there remains a further requirement to consider how they use imaginative language to articulate patterns of belief. This makes them different from other texts you will be studying.

No one has captured the elusive essence of prayer, which at its best is both poetry and interpreter of the story and promise of Scripture, better than George Herbert. His poem entitled 'Prayer (I)' shows how prayer distils all the riches of the tradition into a feast that is a foretaste of heaven itself. It might be made up of a number of fragments of remembered phrases, or a re-imagining of real events in different terms, or all of these things. In the end, though, it is 'something understood', which sounds simple but opens a window onto an extraordinary mystery. Reflecting on the literature of worship in the light of an inheritance of scriptural teaching and belief is also an activity in which something might be understood. It invites us not only to question the texts we pray and sing, but also to pray and sing the questions.

Further reading

Davies, J G (ed.) (1986), *A New Dictionary of Liturgy and Worship*, London, SCM. (This gives useful definitions of terms which may be unfamiliar.)

Dudley, M R (1994), *The Collect in Anglican Liturgy* (Alcuin Club Collections 72), Liturgical Press, Collegeville, Minnesota.

Evans, R (1999), Using words: metaphor and translation, in *Using the Bible: studying the text*, pp. 47–58, London, Darton, Longman and Todd.

Gardner, H (1971), Religious poetry, in *Religion and Literature*, pp. 121–142, Oxford, Oxford University Press.

Jasper, D and Jasper, R (1990), *Language and the Worship of the Church*, Basingstoke, Macmillan.

Finn, P C and Schellman, J M (eds) (1990), *Shaping English Liturgy: studies in honour of Archbishop Denis Hurley*, New York, Pastoral Press. (Recounts Roman Catholic experience of producing modern English liturgy.)

Perham, M (ed.) (1993), *The Renewal of Common Prayer: unity and diversity in Church of England worship*, London, Church House Publishing. (This is helpful on what is important in the tradition.)

The Book of Common Prayer, Cambridge, Cambridge University Press.

4. POETRY OF REDEMPTION

Introduction

The two previous chapters have worked from two possible starting points in students' experience, namely the Bible and some knowledge of patterns of prayer and worship. This chapter returns to another cultural landmark, the work of William Shakespeare, to introduce the kinds of questions that a literary text might raise in the realm of faith.

  📖 **Before embarking on this chapter, you should read Shakespeare's**
     Pericles. If you have the opportunity, listen to an audiotape of the
     play or watch a video. Both of these media will help you to imagine
     the dramatic action and follow the rhythm of the poetry.

    Pericles belongs to a group of four plays, written at the end of Shakespeare's career. The other plays included in this family are *Cymbeline*, *The Winter's Tale* and *The Tempest*. (Some commentators add *Henry VIII* and *The Two Noble Kinsmen*, but this classification presents certain difficulties.) Although they are usually gathered under the term 'romances', the word does not do justice to the complexity of human motive that they explore.

    First in the sequence of four, and not considered one of Shakespeare's great plays, *Pericles* retells the legend of Pericles, Prince of Tyre. It takes us on a journey that is both real and metaphorical, as it follows its hero's progress from his home in Tyre to Antioch, Pentapolis, Tharsus, Mytilene and Ephesus. In the course of his travels, Pericles moves from expectation, to betrayal, to new love, to death and to the rediscovery of life and love. There is a deliberate symmetry about the play's events and this demonstrates a real possibility at the end for evil to be redressed by good, for life to be reclaimed from death, and for love to spring up again when it seemed lost for ever. One of the central questions we will be asking, is whether the play's concern is only with setting right the evils of the past, or whether it has equal or greater bearing on future events that lie beyond the scope of its action.

In the course of reading *Pericles*, we are asked to consider the recovery of a life capable of affirming love and hope after betrayal, misfortune and despair. Much of the play's action consists of reversal of fortunes, tragic dissolution of loving family bonds, threats of violence and descent into mourning. Yet all of these events are eventually redressed in the reunion of loved ones, an apparent resurrection from the dead, the healing of disturbed emotions and the joyful celebration of a marriage. Our reading aims to show that there is more to restoration than simply making things all right in the end. The intervening suffering matters greatly to the final happiness. It has left its mark, without lessening the joy, and has a good deal in common with the sort of faith that can learn from the past, and yet still look forward in hope.

Reflecting on experience

Try to recall an occasion when you have been conscious of returning to happiness after great loss or suffering (perhaps after a death, an illness or the end of a relationship).

Spend some time considering whether you would speak of this experience in terms of 'redemption' or 'resurrection'.

In what respects might you describe the journey from health and happiness, through suffering to renewal, as a pattern?

The reflection you have just performed will have made you think in overarching terms of the course of a whole life, or at least a fairly large part of a life. *Pericles* is, of course, a play with a happy ending, but in order to grasp something of the depth of the happiness that finally materialises, it is important to have grappled with the difficulties that would seem to militate against joy and contentment at every stage in the action.

This is explored through Pericles' fluctuating fortunes, as well as through the contrast between characters who are examples of goodness and characters whose depravity is blatant. The drama presents us with a bewildering variety of places and events in the unfolding of its narrative. But we are enabled to make sense of its leaps across tracts of space and time by two significant linking devices.

Patterning action

First of all, we should consider the careful manipulation of the passage of time through the action of the play. Crucial to this is the character of the medieval poet Gower, who performs the function of a dramatic chorus. Gower's introductions to each shift in the drama often cover the passage of several years. They sketch in details that are necessary for the audience's understanding, but not important enough to merit development in the play itself. The presence of Gower, with his quaint and rather archaic style of speech, also reminds us that *Pericles* is a re-telling of a traditional story. Re-telling often brings new insights. You should therefore be alert to the possibility that this dramatic version may reach beyond the boundaries of the original tale.

Second, there is room for reflection on the manipulation of space. The play's half-imaginary, half-real geographical locations have nothing to link them except the sea, constantly bearing Pericles from one place to another, away from one group of characters and towards a different group. It controls key events, notably the birth of Marina and the apparent death of Thaisa. It assumes the status of a powerful living entity, stronger than any human power, as audiences are reminded when Pericles addresses the storm (Act II, scene i, lines 1–11; Act III, scene i, lines 1–9). Yet it also provides the metaphor to describe Pericles' joy when he meets his daughter after hearing that she has died (Act V, scene i, line 192).

In addition to these powerful background devices, there is a motif in the plot that will demand close attention. The theme I have in mind is the father-daughter bond. For not only does it help us to gain a larger understanding of the events that take place over the period occupied by the action, it actually constitutes these events.

EXERCISE

Make a list of all the father-daughter relationships in the play. As you are doing this, try to classify them as respectively 'wholesome' or 'perverted'.

The table you have constructed probably includes three key relationships, namely the bond between Antiochus and his daughter, the relationship of Simonides and Thaisa, and the relationship of Pericles and Marina. We begin with the first of these, not only because the incestuous transaction between Antiochus and his daughter confronts the audience in the opening scene without any preparation, but also because it will set bearings for the rest of the action.

Incest is an offence against Nature itself. Ancient Gower, whose dramatic function is to conduct us through time, describes it thus:

> Bad child, worse father, to entice his own
> To evil should be done by none.
> But custom what they did begin
> Was with long use account'd no sin.
> (Act I, Prologue, lines 7–30)

As if infected by the poisoned family at Antioch, all the suitors who seek the young woman in the legitimate bond of marriage find themselves doomed to death. As the drama begins, the stage direction tells us that we are 'before the palace of Antioch, with heads displayed above the entrance'. These severed heads testify to the numbers of young men who have not met the conditions for marriage by solving the riddle. For Pericles, who does see the hideous truth, the prospect is hardly more optimistic. It is a game of chance in which the outsider always loses, and Antiochus would prefer to see Pericles dead than fleeing Antioch to betray his secret to the world. (For that is another feature of incest. It is always a secret belonging to the participants.)

EXERCISE

📖 **Re-read the riddle in Act I, scene i, lines 65–72:**

> I am no viper, yet I feed
> On mother's flesh which did me breed.
> I sought a husband, in which labour
> I found that kindness in a father.
> He's father, son and husband mild;
> I mother, wife, and yet his child:
> How they may be, and yet in two,
> As you will live, resolve it you.

What techniques are used here to point to an unnatural relationship?

It will take the rest of the action to retrieve the possibility of a fully restored and wholesome family affection from this ugly travesty of the love of parent and child. But even at an early stage, Pericles meets the beginnings of redemption in Simonides and Thaisa, the father and daughter he meets at Pentapolis.

Act II takes us from Pericles' dejected arrival at Pentapolis, ship-wrecked and in rusty armour, to his marriage with Thaisa. This part of his career shows, point for point, how the father and daughter at Antioch are only the grotesque reflection of something intrinsically good. Thaisa's birthday is to be celebrated with a tournament, where knights from distant places will compete for her hand. She is introduced by her father as 'Beauty's child, whom Nature gat/ For men to see, and seeing wonder at' (Act II, scene ii, lines 6–7). 'Nature' is always an important word in Renaissance literature. It is a bedrock of truth, forming the foundation for a correct view of the world and for sound human relationships. Nature, as represented at Pentapolis, is the antithesis of what Pericles has encountered at Antioch.

As in Antioch, Pericles must face a test imposed by Simonides. This time, however, the premises are honest. Although Simonides seems hostile and anxious to find fault with the prince, his 'asides' (those words spoken by an actor supposedly to himself, so that the audience has access to knowledge not available to other characters) indicate how delighted he is that his daughter should have fallen in love with him. So satisfied is he with Pericles' staunch defence of his honour and good reputation under the pressure of antagonistic questioning, that he insists on a marriage between him and Thaisa (Act II, scene v).

The third significant father-daughter pair arises directly out of this marriage, with the birth of Marina during a storm at sea. This relationship is pivotal to the play's movement from despair to joy.

EXERCISE

📖 **Read Act III, scene i, lines 15–37 and Act V, scene i, lines 1–211.**

These passages mark perhaps the lowest and highest points of Pericles' fortunes. Notice the characters' dominant emotions and the use of language related to the two great themes of birth and death.

The poles of redemption

In the first of the passages examined in the last exercise, we see the beginning of Marina's life overshadowed by her mother's death. Her birth seems to contravene all the laws of Nature. She is delivered from Thaisa's apparently dead body. Twice we are reminded that she was born at sea (Act III, scene iii, line 13; Act V, scene i, lines 155–156). Further, her birth takes place amid the full rage of a storm. Every part of this event runs counter to the patterns of Nature and convention: life emerges out of death; birth is geographically imprecise on the shifting waters of the sea; the usual comforts of light and fire are replaced by the wild conflict of the four elements.

The second passage, fourteen years further on in dramatic time, reverses these disruptions in the normal patterning of human life, but again on terms which threaten to stand Nature on its head. By now, Marina is grown up. Having escaped murder at Tharsus only because pirates kidnapped her under the nose of the would-be assassin, she finds herself resisting the designs of the proprietors of a brothel in Mytilene. At this time, the grieving Pericles, silent and unshaven since he learned of the supposed death of his daughter from the deceitful Cleon and Dionyza at Tharsus, arrives by ship in Mytilene's harbour. His attendants, hearing of Marina's charismatic effect on the local population, suggest that she might draw Pericles out of his great sadness. In the course of their conversation, each discovers the other's identity. Pericles' joy at this moment is boundless – he compares it to a 'great sea of joys rushing upon me' (Act V, scene i, line 192), and it is worth returning to the lines with which he hails Marina:

> O, come hither,
> Thou that beget'st him that did thee beget;
> Thou that wast born at sea, buried at Tharsus,
> And found at sea again. O Helicanus,
> Down on thy knees! thank the holy gods as loud
> As thunder threatens us: this is Marina.
> (Act V, scene i, lines 190–199)

The language of this outburst looks back in a curious way to the disfigured parent-child relationship at Antioch. Antiochus' daughter has usurped her mother's place as childbearer, parent and sexual partner, thus reducing the conventional minimum number of the family unit from three to two. Marina's reunion with her father could be better described as a transfiguration of the bond between father and daughter. The metaphors of death and birth are undeniably extraordinary, unless we accept that Pericles is fully restored to life beyond all expectation by finding his daughter. It is as though he has died of joy and been reborn. To complete the family, the very next scenes take father and daughter to Ephesus, where Thaisa, long believed dead, returns to her husband and child.

Integrity and corruption: the potential of humanity

We will return to these events, bearing in mind what they have to say about resurrection and redemption in the light of the Christian tradition. But before that, it is important to recognise that the condition of humanity, with its potential for corruption and salvation, also comes in less exalted guises during the course of the play. The staff and diseased clients of the brothel in Mytilene provide a comical parade of moral decay and its physical results. Their exaggerated crudeness is emphasised even further by the intrusion of Marina into their midst. In fact, the earthy, slapstick humour of these scenes might be said to be dramatically the most successful feature of *Pericles*.

EXERCISE
📖 **Read again Act IV, scene ii.**

Make a note of the repeated references to rotten flesh (a symptom of venereal disease) and other allusions to the exchange of infection between the brothel and its patrons, for example Monsieur Verolles (line 104). Also look for images of eating and greedy, almost cannibalistic consumption of food (for example lines 128–130).

Why do you think the audience's attention is being so insistently focused upon the degraded elements in Mytilene?

Some forms of corruption, it would seem, are beyond retrieval by good influences. They belong to a type of evil that is self-consuming. In the case of Monsieur Verolles and his like, predatory transactions with the prostitutes in the brothel produce a continuing exchange of infection, leading inevitably to debility and death. To some degree, they parody the grim consumption of unlawful flesh and blood relations that characterises the incestuous pair at Antioch.

Lysimachus, the governor of Mytilene, presents a different possibility. The motives for his visit to Marina are deliberately ambiguous. Is he a regular customer? Has he only come to see the unusual girl whose attractions have been advertised in the town? Certainly, he is well known to the Bawd, the Pandar and Boult, and the audience is alerted to the fact that there may be something furtive or at least mysterious about his mission with the Bawd's announcement:

> Here comes the Lord Lysimachus, disguis'd.
> (Act IV, scene vi, lines 15–16)

The dialogue between Lysimachus and Marina confirms the integrity of both and sets the scene for their eventual marriage. Lysimachus affirms that, even had he brought 'a corrupted mind' with him, he would have been converted to goodness by Marina's words. He insists that he 'came with no ill intent' and goes away promising that Marina will hear from him only to her benefit (Act IV, scene vi, lines 102–116). Whether we believe this presentation of his motives or not, he leaves the brothel with his mind newly directed to honourable action. Marina's wholesome influence spreads in the town where disease has proliferated before. Gower sketches her move to an honest house, where she earns her living by using her skills as a needlewoman (Act V, Chorus, lines 1–11). All of this culminates, of course, in the healing action Marina performs for her father, when she gently and patiently draws him back into the bonds of human communication and indeed into family relationship (Act V, scene i).

More than coincidence?

This moment of recognition draws the play together. It looks back to events that have brought Pericles to Mytilene. Equally, it looks forward to the reconstitution of the family at Ephesus, a place of healing presided over by the priest-king Cerimon. As if to confirm that order has been restored, 'heavenly music' (audible at least to Pericles) rings out (Act V, scene i, line 232), lulling the hero into the sleep that brings a vision of the goddess Diana, summoning the party to Ephesus. At one level, all that remains is for Thaisa to recognise her husband and daughter and join in blessing Marina's marriage to Lysimachus. The play has thus gone through a complete cycle.

EXERCISE

How would you sum up the lessons that have been taught, if we were to approach *Pericles* as the tale of a cycle of human experience that eventually returns its exemplary characters to happiness? In other words, try to state the moral of the story.

In the exercise above, you have been asked to treat the play as a moral fable. You might legitimately have mentioned the testing of love and faithfulness and the rebirth of hope out of despair, and observations along these lines certainly reveal one approach to interpreting the drama. Yet you may feel that to ask the action to bear much of a didactic burden is stretching the plot beyond its capacity. We have not, after all, discussed the marked presence of coincidence in the plot. The journey from Tharsus, covered briefly in Gower's prologue to Act II, conveniently ends in a shipwreck that washes Pericles up in Pentapolis. This facilitates his marriage with Thaisa, who is in turn the subject of a fortunate turn that deposits her coffin on the shores of Ephesus. Years later, having travelled to Tharsus to reclaim Marina, only to learn that she is dead, Pericles breaks his homeward journey at Mytilene. There is no narrative reason for this, but as it happens Marina has herself been brought there by pirates. Their reunion, culminating in a divine visitation from Diana, directs them to Tharsus, where Thaisa proves, miraculously, to be alive.

On the one hand, coincidence is often frowned upon as a weakness in the construction of literary plots. Certainly, it can be used to avoid the challenges of pursuing a course of events towards an ending that has to be plausibly accounted for at every stage in the process. On the other hand, coincidence may be a favoured ploy where the credibility of a plot is not the first preoccupation of a literary work. In this case, it is a vehicle that brings together widely separated elements into a coherent whole. It overrides the constraints of time and space in the interests of restoring order, joy and dignity to human life. And the fact that some of the occurrences are far-fetched adds to, rather than detracts from, the vision of the play. For, as Kiernan Ryan has argued, the late 'romances', of which *Pericles* is one, look forward rather than backward. Their aim is not simply the restoration of a former order but also the desire for a better order, that has not yet been achieved. By using the well-known techniques of storytelling that belong to the world of 'once upon a time', they are familiar enough in shape to allow us to be receptive to the almost prophetic hopefulness of their resolutions.

The following passage offers an interpretation of *Pericles* that you should read carefully in the light of your own conclusions about the play:

> The symbolically condensed projections of Shakespearean romance allow us to grasp the potential as if it were already actual, to watch the improbable and the impossible become plausible and feasible before our very eyes. By repeatedly treating us to tales in which 'wishes fall out as they're will'd' (*Pericles*, V, ii, 16), these plays seek to break the cynical grip of realism on our minds and sustain the insatiable hunger of hope, our yearning for the world to be otherwise. (Ryan, 1999, p.16)

Listening to the tradition

A 'yearning for the world to be otherwise' might find many different ways to express itself. Such longings have underwritten political movements, humanitarian projects, great literary and artistic works, and developments in engineering and architecture. None of these necessarily presupposes a Christian foundation, although the Christian tradition, too, is committed to bringing about a world that is 'otherwise'. What enables us to claim that Christianity is different and that, in addition to a vision for this world, it reaches out to something more?

One of the most important differences between Christian belief and purely humanitarian ideology is that the Christian framework is eschatological. It turns to the promises of Scripture for the assurance of salvation and the coming of the Kingdom of God. Thus, looking backwards to the Old Testament, it finds the repeated signs of God's covenanted faithfulness with his chosen people. Looking forward again through the New Testament, it discovers the pointers to the eternal Kingdom as they are set out in the ministry of Jesus. These promises are brought to mind regularly in the sacramental life of the Christian community, especially in baptism and the celebration of the Eucharist.

Pericles, though it takes place in a semi-mythological world governed by pagan gods, is built on a thematic plan that asks us to concentrate on eschatological questions. It works out the concerns of life and death, loss and recovery, chaos and order, through lively action. At the close of the play, both Marina and Thaisa are miraculously restored to Pericles and political order returns to the imaginary region, this time consolidated by the marriage of Marina and Lysimachus. There are a number of biblical *types* to which we might refer in reflecting on these events in the light of the Christian tradition. (Chapter 7 will give you an opportunity to study the device of typology.)

Life restored from death is an image that can be traced through Old and New Testament narrative. Joseph, cast into a well and left for dead by his brothers (Genesis 37), Jonah emerging against all odds from the belly of the whale (Jonah 1 and 2), the Prodigal Son (Luke 15:11–32), the raising of Lazarus (John 11) and the recovery of Jairus' daughter (Matthew 9:18–26; Mark 5:22–43; Luke 8:41–56) all establish a pattern that the tradition has seen in the light of the resurrection of Jesus himself. A variation on the shift from death to recovery is to be found in the story of Job. His faithfulness in the face of astonishing suffering ends in the renewal of happiness and the reconstitution of human bonds.

Another biblical genre that shares the interests of recovery, renewal and restoration, is the group of parables of the Kingdom. The philosopher Paul Ricoeur has described some of them as working according to 'a logic of superabundance' (Ricoeur, 1975, p. 138).

📖 **Read Matthew 13:31–33.** In this passage we hear through the language of parable that there is always more in the divine promise than could possibly have been hoped for. The mustard seed yields a great tree and a little yeast raises a whole batch of dough. Again, Matthew 17:20 tells how faith no bigger than a mustard seed can move mountains. In other parables, notably the story of the Prodigal Son (Luke 15) and the story of the woman who finds a lost coin (Luke 15:8–9), loss is overturned by the joy of reunion or rediscovery.

Certainly, all of these narratives conclude with a restitution of earthly order within the scale of mortal time. But, more importantly, they point beyond themselves, whether as types of resurrection or as snapshots that try to capture something of the infinite generosity of the Kingdom of Heaven. In all cases, they express life-changing events, sometimes seeming to defy logic, or at least displacing human logic in favour of the logic of the Kingdom. This is sharply focused in the dilemma facing the lawyer Nicodemus, who approaches Jesus by night asking how he might enter the Kingdom. He is astonished to hear that he must be born again (John 3).

In that light, we should turn, finally, to the events of birth and being

POETRY OF REDEMPTION 47

born again that feature throughout *Pericles*. Antiochus' daughter's riddle hints perversely that she is both child and mother to her father;
Marina's birth at sea assures a corrected version of the incestuous
family at Antioch; and Thaisa's landing at Ephesus is, in a sense, a birth
out of the sea. Finally, there is Pericles' own claim to have been brought
to birth again through the kindness of his own daughter (Act V, scene i,
lines 194–195). Such a birth can only look forward. It places characters
in a restored but changed relationship to one another, in a world that is
differently configured.

It would be limiting the richness of the play to read it in the end as a
Christian parable. What it shows us is how concerns that lie at the heart
of Christian belief can be addressed in other voices. We are invited to
encounter it on its own terms first and foremost but also, challenged by
its address to good and evil, birth, death, resurrection and redemption,
invited to see the tradition itself in a new light.

Further reading

Bloom, H (1999), Pericles, in *Shakespeare: the invention of the human*,
pp. 603–613, London, Fourth Estate.
Kermode, F (1963), *Shakespeare: the final plays* (Writers and Their Work, no. 155),
London, Longman.
Ryan, K (ed.) (1999), *Shakespeare: the last plays*, London and New York, Longman.

5. DESPAIR AND DEATH

Introduction

Pericles shows the possibility of renewal, of consolation for those who keep faith with themselves and others, and even of a new world for the family it reunites. Its depiction of suffering is completed, in other words, by a powerful shift to joy. But what of those for whom suffering is an unanswerable condition?

This chapter moves from the uncertainty that can be resolved, to the bleakness of despair and the fear of death. It introduces students to the way that these conditions have been voiced in the work of two poets. Gerard Manley Hopkins articulates the barrenness and desperation felt by a believer who finds it impossible to communicate with God. Philip Larkin, on the other hand, refuses any of the consolations of faith in describing confrontations with death and the conviction that beyond it there is only oblivion.

Students might wonder what place Larkin's denial of any redemptive hope, however remote, has in a book like this. In reply, it should be said that the discussion of literature and religion is not a closed one, admitting only those who will confess to religious belief of some kind. The absence of faith or belief is a condition that cannot be wished away. It is always there as a possibility inherent in faith itself and it continues to assert its right to be represented in literature.

Reflecting on experience
Have you reached moments in your own life when you felt afflicted by any of the following: no sense of purpose, no sense of cumulative achievement, separation from all the reference points that conventionally give meaning to human existence ▶▶

(for example friendship, loving family relationships, enjoyment of the created world), separation even from God?

How did you react under these conditions, and what resources did you turn to in the attempt to resolve the situation?

The states you have been asked to reflect on come within the experience of most human beings to some degree, at one or other time in their lives. The Christian faith acknowledges and addresses such feelings. But it would be wrong to caricature it as offering quick and easy answers. Sometimes the test of faith lies in enduring long tracts of spiritual darkness. For those who have rejected the claims of faith altogether, another kind of endurance is demanded, unrelated to any possibility of redemptive change.

Enduring darkness

Read Gerard Manley Hopkins' sonnet, 'I wake and feel the fell of dark':

I wake and feel the fell of dark, not day.
What hours, O what black hours we have spent
This night! what sights you, heart, saw; ways you went!
And more must, in yet longer light's delay.
    With witness I speak this. But where I say
Hours I mean years, mean life. And my lament
Is cries countless, cries like dead letters sent
To dearest him that lives alas! away.

  I am gall, I am heartburn. God's most deep decree
Bitter would have me taste: my taste was me;
Bones built in me, flesh filled, blood brimmed the curse.
    Selfyeast of spirit a dull dough sours. I see
The lost are like this, and their scourge to be
As I am mine, their sweating selves; but worse.

EXERCISE
This poem belongs to a group of Hopkins' poems known as the 'terrible sonnets'. Reflect on the qualities of description and emotion that make this an apt description.

The exercise you have just performed will also have helped you to imagine the dramatic setting of the poem. It comes out of the meditation of several sleepless hours before dawn, and very quickly moves from what might be one incident to a whole weary pattern of futile occupation and personal despair. Yet this is not the poem's last word. We might describe it as a negative affirmation of faith, for in the midst of pervading spiritual darkness that swamps the speaker, he knows the presence of God, albeit in separation.

One of the devices that the poem uses is the form of dialogue. Here, the participants in the conversation are the speaker and his own heart. In descriptions of religious experience, the heart often appears equivalent to the soul. It is, metaphorically, the emotionally sensitive, affective part of the human being. But it is also the organ associated with loving response to God. Both Old and New Testaments refer repeatedly to the heart in this way.

It is, therefore, a source of great grief to the speaker that the heart seems unable to communicate with God and that instead it sends out 'cries countless, cries like dead letters sent/ To dearest him that lives alas! away'.

EXERCISE
📖 **Carefully re-read the first eight lines (octave) of the sonnet.**

Try to notice the linguistic strategies that enable the speaker to articulate weariness, frustration, the slow passage of time and the inexpressible distress that has built up over a period of spiritual barrenness. Pay particular attention to alliteration, repetition and internal rhyme.

Hopkins' writing is extremely rich and dense, and you will often find that a single word has multiple meanings attached to it. Look for some examples of this.

Your list probably includes all or some of the following observations. The first line uses the alliterative pair, 'feel' and 'fell', to suggest the oppressive character of the night. 'Fell' is the past participle of 'fall', and thus reminds us of nightfall itself. It is also an adjective meaning 'evil'. This secondary resonance underpins the speaker's experience of night as an evil time, when he is most vulnerable to attacks of doubt and a conviction of the worthlessness of his life. The repetition of 'hours' in line 2, strengthened the second time by the adjective 'black', conveys the interminable length of this wakeful time, and the alliterating 'w' sound (lines 3–5) gathers up all the woeful anguish of this into the texture of the verse. Despair becomes most intensely focused in line 6, where the speaker finally admits that the long hours are really no different from a long, empty, searching, mourning life. The line breaks tangibly at the full stop, to be followed only by lament. This the poem conveys in the sharp hard 'c' sounds ('cries countless, cries'), but also in the sobbing 'l's of 'lament', 'countless', 'letters', 'lives' and 'alas'. The octave ends on a dying wail – the weak last syllable of 'away'.

An often contorted and cumbersome arrangement of words supports these methods of slowing the poem down and creating internal impediments to mimic the slow passing of the early hours of the morning. Lines 3–4 are excellent examples of this device, as are the repetitions in lines 2, 6 and 7.

EXERCISE

As you sum up your close examination of the octave, devote time to discussing the power of the simile, 'cries like dead letters'.

What does this image have to say about a desirable relationship with God?

What seemingly unconventional or even inappropriate comparisons does the simile evoke?

The last six lines (sestet) of the sonnet turn from a description of symptoms to a diagnosis. The speaker characterises the bitterness of his grief in separation from God as the burning acid of violent indigestion: 'I am gall, I am heartburn.' Why should God inflict this on his own creature? The answer seems to be that the inescapable suffering, formed out of the sufferer's own being ('my taste was me;/ Bones built in me, flesh filled, blood brimmed the curse') is a way of waking up a spirit that had ceased to feel any lively response.

Self-generating apathy has to be corrected by timely self-recognition. Just as it is possible to make bread by turning the dough sour to make it rise, so the determined spirit can regenerate itself: 'Selfyeast of spirit a dull dough sours.' It would appear that this lesson has been learned just in time. The speaker still has some ability to assess his own situation, and to see how close it is to a condition that defies any redemption.

EXERCISE
In the light of the paragraph above, spend some time reflecting on the last three lines ('I see/ The lost . . . but worse'). What is the difference between the speaker and 'the lost'?

Listening to the tradition

This poem speaks of the darkest kind of despondency and failure to find spiritual consolation and the evidence points to a long-term condition. At the same time, it never gives up its acknowledgement of God, even though the God of the poem is a God known only in absence. The speaker continues to see his futile hours, and even his whole life of cries and laments, as ongoing but unsuccessful attempts to communicate with God.

Scripture offers a well-defined paradigm for this condition in a number of the Psalms. Psalm 130 begins with the agonised words, 'Out of the depths have I cried unto thee, O Lord', and goes on to urge the wisdom of waiting for God to act. 'My soul waiteth for the Lord', says the psalmist, 'more than they that watch for the morning.' This psalm belongs to a group called the penitential psalms which includes Psalms 6, 32, 38, 51, 102 and 143. To this category you might add Psalm 22. All of them are worth reading as analogues of the kind of despair that confronts us in 'I wake and feel the fell of dark', especially because they hold to the possibility that despair can be resolved, and that God will intervene. It is significant that in Mark's gospel Jesus quotes Psalm 22 on the cross: 'My God, my God, why have you forsaken me?' (Matthew 27:46). A little later, we learn that one of the bystanders offered Jesus vinegar on a sponge to quench his thirst (Mark 15:34–36). The hope of resurrection is temporarily eclipsed, but it is not extinguished. It is useful to remember, if we are to refer to a typology of resurrection out of darkness, hopelessness and death, that it is in the light of the early morning that Mary Magdalene comes upon the risen Christ in the garden (John 20:10–18).

Mary's discovery was a moment of disbelief, followed by ecstasy, catapulting her from the depths of grief to a joy she had not believed she would experience again. It is an image that you might keep in mind, as you reflect once more on the earlier exercise which asked you to think broadly about the nature of the speaker's relationship with God. You may have decided that the end of the octave suggests the pain of a deserted lover, who goes on writing letters that are either not delivered or never answered. The question is, whether this is a suitable way of imagining the soul's relationship to God.

The tradition of Christian spirituality shows us many examples of individuals whose passion for God found expression in a language usually reserved for lovers, with all the variations between ecstasy and despair that mark the emotional flux of passionate relationships. 'I wake and feel the fell of dark' does not rule out joy in its cry of misery. If only the unresponsive beloved would answer the 'dead letters', we feel, things might change. But in the substance of the poem, this is an agony to be lived with, not resolved.

The impossibility of consolation: death and the other

📖 Read Philip Larkin's 'Myxomatosis':

> Caught in the centre of a soundless field
> While hot inexplicable hours go by
> *What trap is this? Where were its teeth concealed?*
> You seem to ask.
>   I make a short reply,
> Then clean my stick. I'm glad I can't explain
> Just in what jaws you were to suppurate:
> You might have thought things would come right again
> If you could only keep quite still and wait.

EXERCISE

To make sense of this poem, you will find it useful to imagine the dramatic setting. In particular, reflect on the identity of the speaker, and the identity of the questioner who is puzzled about the hidden trap.

It will help you to know that myxomatosis is a fatal viral disease producing oozing tumours, artificially developed originally to control the rabbit population in Australia. It spread more widely than intended, and the kind of death it produced was slow and cruel.

Perhaps the picture you have in mind is something like this: the speaker comes upon a dying rabbit in a field. Realising what is wrong with the creature, and knowing the painful and irreversible consequences, he delivers a swift blow to its head. In this instance, killing seems kinder than prolonged suffering that would in any case end in death. The action is justified by the fact that the speaker has superior knowledge of the inevitable results of the disease. The suffering animal, on the other hand, has no insight into its own condition, and thus lies passively waiting for things to 'come right again'.

The speaker's decision could be described as rational and humane without reference to the feelings he imagines the rabbit expressing. It is given a different slant, however, because he anthropomorphises the rabbit. Anthropomorphism is a technical term for attributing human characteristics, especially speech, thought and emotional sophistication, to animals. In this poem, the use of this technique puts the rabbit on an almost equal footing with the speaker. The creature can think and feel. The only difference is that it cannot fully understand why it is suffering. Its imagined question, 'What trap is this? Where were its teeth concealed?' therefore opens up the possibility of an answer. But in this case the answer, or 'reply', is a euphemism for a brutal, non-verbal action. There is no real conversation here, only a decision based on the belief that quick death is the lesser of two evils. Death itself is a foregone conclusion.

EXERCISE

Now that you have performed one sort of attentive reading of the poem, consider it again.

Is it simply a poem about a sick rabbit and the human being who ends its predicament?

Could its terms be extended to embrace the suffering of all innocent victims and the decisions of those who try to find the only solutions possible in situations that cannot be redeemed?

To support your conclusions, you will need to be able to refer to the literary techniques that have enabled the poem to achieve its effects. Care has been taken to evoke a world of silence, unable to give answers to questions. The field is 'soundless', except for the alliterative 's' sound which might be nothing more than a rustling of grass ('centre', 'soundless'). The silence is completely unresponsive. Even the hours are 'inexplicable' and the sense of a limitless time with no purpose to fill it is made more emphatic by the unusual adjective. An 'inexplicable' predicament might mean something. 'Inexplicable hours' catch time and events into meaningless misery. And so in this case, the whole environment becomes responsible for the lack of an answer to the rabbit's imagined question. An abrupt change of mood breaks the stillness, however. The harsh sounds of the alliterating 't' in 'trap' and 'teeth' intrude savagely on the quiet scene, and the equally abrupt line-break ('You seem to ask./ I make a sharp reply') reinforces the effect. The unusual full stop in mid-line that follows makes a clear break between the act of killing, with its clinical conclusion ('Then clean my stick') and the speaker's final self-justifying reflection.

Listening to the tradition

When is it right to kill? Who has the power to decide how much suffering is enough?

The scriptural tradition offers us more case histories than you might think at first. You might consider the story of Job, and even Samson's treatment under the Philistines (Judges 16:18–31). The Psalms, especially Psalms 22, 69 and 70, speak of the anguish of those who feel separated from God and unable to find a way out of their distress. Jesus himself, both in the Garden of Gethsemane and on the cross, reveals the terror of lonely agony. Nowhere are the hours following the Last Supper more poignantly described than in Luke's gospel (Luke 22:39–46). Matthew stresses the desolation Jesus felt on the cross (Matthew 27:45–49). All of these events, though, are somehow modulated by reference to subsequent triumph or salvation. Job is restored to prosperity. Samson overcomes the Philistines in the end. The psalmist knows that in the direst misery, God can rescue him. Jesus rises from the dead and ascends to his Father.

There is perhaps only one event which is consistent with the event described in 'Myxomatosis', and this is Herod's massacre of infant boys in his determination to prevent the child born to be King of the Jews from taking his throne (Matthew 2:16–18). Both are instances of the vindictive persecution of the innocent. Neither sees any hope of redemption.

'The total emptiness forever': death and the self

📖 Read Philip Larkin's 'Aubade'. (An aubade is, properly, a poem or piece of music to greet the dawn. The word comes from the French word for 'dawn', which is *aube*.)

I work all day, and get half-drunk at night.
Waking at four to soundless dark, I stare.
In time the curtain-edges will grow light.
Till then I see what's really always there:
Unresting death, a whole day nearer now,
Making all thought impossible but how
And where and when I shall myself die.
Arid interrogation: yet the dread
Of dying, and being dead,
Flashes afresh to hold and horrify.

The mind blanks at the glare. Not in remorse
– The good not done, the love not given time
Torn off unused – nor wretchedly because
An only life can take so long to climb
Clear of its wrong beginnings, and may never;
But at the total emptiness for ever,
The sure extinction that we travel to
And shall be lost in always. Not to be here,
Not to be anywhere,
And soon; nothing more terrible, nothing more true.

This is a special way of being afraid
No trick dispels. Religion used to try,
That vast moth-eaten musical brocade
Created to pretend we never die,
And specious stuff that says *No rational being*
Can fear a thing it will not feel, not seeing
That this is what we fear – no sight, no sound,
No touch or taste or smell, nothing to think with,
Nothing to love or link with,
The anaesthetic from which none come round.

And so it stays just on the edge of vision,
A small unfocused blur, a standing chill

That slows each impulse down to indecision.
Most things may never happen: this one will,
And realisation of it rages out
In furnace-fear when we are caught without
People or drink. Courage is no good:
It means not scaring others. Being brave
Lets no one off the grave.
Death is no different whined at than withstood.

Slowly light strengthens, and the room takes shape.
It stands plain as a wardrobe, what we know,
Have always known, know that we can't escape,
Yet can't accept. One side will have to go.
Meanwhile telephones crouch, getting ready to ring
In locked-up offices, and all the uncaring
Intricate rented world begins to rouse.
The sky is white as clay, with no sun.
Work has to be done.
Postmen like doctors go from house to house.

EXERCISE
Reflect on the mismatch between the situation the poem describes
and its title. Why do you think Larkin chose such a seemingly
inappropriate title? Do you detect any element of humour in the
choice?

The romantic title is a splendid example of *irony*. As you will have
discovered already, it emphasises the poem's depiction of fear and
inevitability by hinting at the conventional way of greeting the morning
with joy and optimism. This is precisely what is absent in 'Aubade'. In
this way, it sets the tone for the dramatic situation: a meditation on
mortality, in the dark silent hours between 4 am and daybreak.

All the evidence suggests that speaker is a lonely, solitary individual,
but that may not be true. There is a great difference between the physical loneliness of someone who lives alone, and the existential loneliness
of someone who may spend a considerable amount of time with other
people and yet feel no bond or connection with them.

What we do know about the speaker is that there is an unvarying rou-
tine governing his existence. 'I work all day, and get half-drunk at night',

he informs us. This cycle is set in a larger cycle of life that is largely wasted ('The good not done, the love not given, time/ Torn off unused') and progresses further and further towards the certainty of death, 'The sure extinction that we travel to'.

In all of this, the only emotion which is sharp, clear and new is the fear of death, especially when it arises away from the temporary distractions of work or the numbing effect of alcohol: 'This is a special way of being afraid/ No trick dispels.' And for those left to face it unshielded, the result is a raging 'furnace-fear'. Part of the anger, we sense, comes out of the attempts – rational and religious – to provide steady consolation in the face of death.

EXERCISE
In the light of your reading of the whole poem, and especially of stanza 3, try to diagnose what is wrong with the conventional arguments against the fear of death (religion's promise of eternal life and the rational proposition that there is nothing frightening in something one does not feel).

The speaker's reaction seems extraordinarily angry, given that he is addressing something inevitable. Yet when we review the development of the poem, and the narrative it weaves around what seems to be a repeated pre-dawn waking nightmare, something striking emerges. These dark hours have no structures around them. There are no visible shapes to map the environment of the bedroom. There are no ordinary routines of working, eating or drinking laid down for a time when one should be asleep. In fact, it is a time when there should be no consciousness at all. These boundaries around our lives are not normally part of our conscious processes, but when they are taken away they leave us undefended from our own thoughts. In other words, the world of the imagination ceases to have controlling limits and we can pursue our own fears almost infinitely.

EXERCISE
You might pause here and compare the human speaker of 'Aubade' with the rabbit-victim of 'Myxomatosis'. What difference does consciousness of the real state of affairs make to the human speaker?

The final stanza restores the bearings of ordinary days: light, shape, work, communication. But this world has changed through the terrifying meditation of the night. The world has become a prison of 'locked–up offices'; it is stalked by predators in the shape of telephones that 'crouch, getting ready to ring' (the last word so close to 'spring'); it is a place of temporary rights, a 'rented world'; and even the postmen are bearers of the news of death as they go 'like doctors . . . from house to house'.

Does the tradition have anything to say?

The Christian tradition draws on a number of texts that assert the resurrection. Perhaps the best known is Jesus' promise that he is 'the resurrection and the life' (John 11:25–26). Paul's moving celebration of the resurrection of the body in 1 Corinthians 15 is as well known as this. Passages from Job (1:21; 19:25–27) and 1 Timothy 6:7 are also taken as expressions of confidence in God's power to redeem humanity into eternity.

The Jewish tradition has a different view of the end of mortal life. The Psalms speak repeatedly of the 'pit' or the shadowy realm of Sheol. Psalms 28:1; 30:9; 39:13; 88:4 and 143:7 all refer in various ways to the fear of oblivion, of going down into the pit. Other references to this place of non-being are to be found in Isaiah (14:15 and 38:17) and Ezekiel (26:20 and 32:18). This goes hand in hand, though, with a sense of urgency about taking action during life on earth. Knowing that the end of existence here is the end of all existence impels the devout believer to use the God-given opportunities within the available limits. This, again, is a point of divergence from our speaker. His sense of the bitter futility of existence, and his view of life as a series of shabby evasions of the reality of death, impede action.

Neither of these perspectives on the end of life and what follows is of the slightest interest to the speaker of 'Aubade'. The Christian hope seems merely part of the 'vast moth-eaten musical brocade/ Created to pretend we never die', while the conviction that death really is the end becomes not an incentive to use this life well, but a continual 'standing chill/ That slows each impulse down to indecision'. If we are going to read with integrity, then we may not force cheerfully redemptive interpretations on such statements, or dismiss them as of no importance to our own situation. In this situation, any further reflection can only be an ongoing meditation on difference, never an attempt to reduce it to sameness – to diagnose Hopkins as temporarily depressed or Larkin as a closet Christian experimenting with unbelief. And that begins a conversation that is as much a task of self-examination for the reader, as a reading of a poem.

Further reading

Editions

If your reading of these poems has made you want to read more of Hopkins' and Larkin's writing, consult the following:

Feeney, P (ed.) (1994), *Hopkins: Selected Poems*, Oxford, Oxford University Press.

Gardner, W H (ed.) (1953), *Poems and Prose of Gerard Manley Hopkins*, Harmondsworth, Penguin.

Thwaite, A (ed.) (1988), *Collected Poems of Philip Larkin*, London, Faber.

Biography

Motion, A (1993), *Philip Larkin: a writer's life*, London, Faber.

White, N (1992), *Hopkins: a literary biography*, Oxford, Clarendon.

Criticism

Alter, R (1990), *The Art of Biblical Poetry*, Edinburgh, T and T Clark.

Bayley, J (1987), *The Order of Battle at Trafalgar and Other Essays*, London, Collins Harvill. (This includes an excellent essay on Larkin.)

Everett, B (1991), *Poets in Their Time: essays on English poetry from Donne to Larkin*, Oxford, Clarendon Press. (This is very useful on Larkin.)

Schmidt, M (1999), *Lives of the Poets*, London, Phoenix. (This includes Larkin and Hopkins.)

Whitehead, J (1995), *Hardy to Larkin: seven English poets*, Munslow, Shropshire, Hearthstone. (This also covers Larkin and Hopkins.)

6. SPEAKING OF GOD IN POETRY

Introduction

Communicating experience, particularly experience that speaks of our relationship with God, might appear to demand the very simplest and clearest of language. The poet William Blake, for example, crystallises the possibility of sensing the presence of God all around us when he writes of seeing 'a World in a Grain of Sand/ And a Heaven in a Wild Flower' ('Auguries of Innocence', lines 1–2; in Blake, 1977, p. 506). These are complex ideas, yet they can be framed in terms that are immediately understood because they draw on our knowledge of ordinary things.

At another level, however, the task of the theological imagination is to describe the indescribable: perhaps a personal sense of extraordinary closeness to God or a powerful insight into God's presence in, and purpose for the world. In this chapter, we turn our attention to the possibility of achieving that ambition in poetic language.

Reflecting on experience

Try to recall an occasion when you have had a feeling that God was very close to you in a tangible way, or when you have been led to think about a vast subject (such as creation, death or eternal life) in the surroundings of a particular building or garden or some other place. Can you say why it is easy or difficult to describe that experience? Do you find it easier to relate it by using pictorial language that relies heavily on the use of the senses?

The challenge to the writer, faced with conveying experiences that have a great deal in common with mystery, is to find new ways of using language. Words have to be able to conjure up pictures, so that readers and listeners can, in turn, make vivid associations between abstract ideas and striking illustrations that help to explain them.

George Herbert wrote a poem called 'The Windows' which used the image of stained-glass church windows to ask questions about the human ability to preach God's word with any kind of credibility. How can human beings, who are themselves 'brittle, crazy' fragments of glass, incapable of letting the light of truth shine through them, possibly be vehicles of God's grace? The answer is that God writes the story of salvation on the damaged human soul and makes it like a high quality window, that shows its own colours better the more light it admits. In this way, 'doctrine and life, colours and light' can become one entity, because all are used for the single purpose of letting God speak through them.

We would probably not have thought of such a comparison without prompting, yet faced with the example, it is hard to think of a better way of explaining how the whole person of the preacher must be involved in ministry.

Metaphysical poetry

The poems you will study in this chapter all belong to the school of seventeenth-century poetry known as metaphysical. Both of the examples are devotional poems, but secular subjects, especially erotic love, crop up just as frequently. In fact, the metaphysical school delighted in crossing boundaries and fusing unrelated objects. Hence the secular language of love and passion often finds its way into religious verse, and the language of religious devotion becomes a vehicle for articulating profound and almost worshipful romantic love.

The appreciation of this kind of poetry lapsed through the eighteenth and nineteenth centuries. Dr Johnson remarked disapprovingly in 1779 that in it, 'the most heterogeneous ideas are yoked by violence together' (Johnson, 1971). It was T S Eliot who revisited and challenged Johnson's judgement in an essay called 'The Metaphysical Poets' (1921). Eliot found in the seventeenth-century poets a uniquely close connection between experience and thought. 'When a poet's mind is perfectly equipped for its work', he argued, 'it is constantly amalgamating disparate experience.' He went on to say that 'in the poet's mind, these experiences are always forming new wholes'. Eliot also praised the poets of this school for their startlingly original use of language and imagery, which succeeds against the odds (Eliot, 1972, p. 287). For example, in a poem called 'Easter', George Herbert compares the sinews of Christ's tortured body, stretched out on the cross, with the strings of a musical instrument:

> His stretched sinews taught all strings, what key
> Is best to celebrate this most high day.

To sum up this sketch, then, the characteristics you will encounter are striking and unexpected images; intricate word order; surprising yet apparently simple solutions to insoluble problems; passionate immediacy in the expression of personal spiritual experience, and a powerful placing of this experience within the great frame of salvation history. In some cases, even the layout or typographical shape of the poem plays its part in the act of expression. Herbert's 'Easter Wings' and 'The Altar' are well-known instances of the pattern poem. We are working, then, with a remarkably rich, flexible and diverse medium. The more you read, the more readily you will begin to see comparisons of technique and style.

📖 **Read Henry Vaughan's 'The Waterfall':**

> With what deep murmurs through time's silent stealth
> Doth thy transparent, cool and wat'ry wealth
> > Here flowing fall,
> > And chide, and call,
> As if his liquid, loose retinue stayed,
> Ling'ring, and were of this steep place afraid,
> > The common pass
> > Where, clear as glass,
> > All must descend
> > Not to an end:
> But quickened by this deep and rocky grave,
> Rise to a longer course more bright and brave.
>
> > Dear stream! dear bank, where often I
> > Have sate, and pleased my pensive eye,
> > Why, since each drop of thy quick store
> > Runs thither, whence it flowed before,
> > Should poor souls fear a shade or night,
> > Who came (sure) from a sea of light?
> > Or since those drops are all sent back
> > So sure to thee, that none doth lack,
> > Why should frail flesh doubt any more
> > That what God takes, he'll not restore?

O useful element and clear!
My sacred wash and cleanser here,
My first consigner unto those
Fountains of life where the Lamb goes!
What sublime truths, and wholesome themes,
Lodge in thy mystical, deep streams!
Such as dull man can never find
Unless that Spirit lead his mind,
Which first upon thy face did move,
And hatched all with his quick'ning love.
As this loud brook's incessant fall
In streaming rings restagnates all,
Which reach by course the bank, and then
Are no more seen, just so pass men.
O my invisible estate,
My glorious liberty, still late!
Thou art the channel my soul seeks,
Not this with cataracts and creeks.

Shape, language and meaning

'The Waterfall' is a poem that speaks at several levels. These reveal themselves as the speaker's gaze moves from the contemplation of the waterfall as a part of the landscape, to the deeper contemplation of the human soul on its journey through earthly life and towards God.

EXERCISE

You will notice that the typographical layout of the first ten lines, which are, if you like, the most literal lines in the poem, is unusual and different from the remaining lines. In the light of the title, think of possible reasons for this.

Both the title and the physical shape of the poem reinforce its use of the waterfall as a governing metaphor. By that, I mean a single metaphor that is capable of being explored from a number of angles to develop a complex argument. You will have noticed how the attributes of the waterfall – its constant flow, its composition out of innumerable tiny drops of water, its fall from a height and its rocky channel – contribute to a wide-ranging approach to a single question: Why should the soul, and particularly the speaker's soul, fear death and the end of life on earth? The way that question is posed and answered in the dramatic context of the speaker's meditation beside the waterfall will shape our discussion of the poem.

The first six lines are an evocative description of the motion of the waterfall. There is a surprising variation in the manner and speed of the water's flow. The picture that is conjured up suggests a smooth, tranquil current suddenly arrested at the point where the channel ends in a sheer drop. You will notice that the differences are not merely observed: they are taken to have an emotional significance that is part of the very nature of the waterfall. In other words, the waterfall is being personified or given the attributes properly belonging to human beings.

EXERCISE

The following words provide clues to the use of personification in the poem: 'murmurs', 'chide', 'call', 'ling'ring', 'afraid'. How do they record changes of mood? Do you find this a persuasive way of conveying the experience of watching a waterfall?

You might also concentrate on the alliterative use of 'l' in 'liquid', 'loose' and 'ling'ring', paying attention to the mimicry of the sound of flowing water. Try to describe the effect this has on your ability to imagine the scene that gives rise to the poem.

Reading Nature

Lines 7–12 explain that, although the edge ('this steep place') seems frightening to the hesitant water drops, it leads in fact to a universal and regenerative destination. Paradoxically, what looks like a 'deep and rocky grave' is really a place of resurrection, where the river continues its journey as a stronger stream, 'a longer course more bright and brave'.

This paradox in Nature prepares the way for an analogy with the life-cycle of the human soul. If the individual drops that make up the waterfall flow to the sea, and through the cycle of condensation and precipitation find their way back eventually to their original springs, why should it not be the same for the soul? Like the water, the speaker suggests, souls begin in the sea, only this time it is the metaphorical sea of heaven, described as an expanse of glass or crystal in Revelation 4:6 and 15:2. Just as each drop is conserved in the natural cycle, there is a divine principle of conservation (perhaps more properly termed salvation) that assures the soul's life after the death of the body. It is prefigured in Job 1:21, which accepts that it is God's purpose to give life and to take it away. St Matthew's gospel promises that God keeps a rigorous account of creation. He knows the fall of every sparrow and the number of hairs on every human head (Matthew 10:29–30).

EXERCISE

Review the development of the comparison between the waterfall and the life of the soul up to the break at line 22. Do you feel that you are in possession of enough evidence to be persuaded by the argument for faith in God's promise of eternal life? If you are not satisfied, try to think of further elements which seem to be missing from the discussion so far.

Lines 23 to the end move the poem from an analogy for salvation to a more adventurous and sophisticated celebration of water as a traditional symbol of salvation, and as a crucial part of the narrative of creation. First, there is a three-stage movement from water as a practical means of washing the body, to water as the symbolic vehicle of baptism ('my *first* consigner unto those/ fountains of life'), to water as the fountain of life to which Christ the Lamb of God will lead the redeemed at the end of time (Revelation 7:17). So we have encountered the natural and ordinary world, the sacramental world of Christian life and worship, and the eschatological understanding of resurrection into new life with Christ. No wonder, then, that the speaker is forced to pause in astonishment at the power of a simple element like water to give access to deep spiritual insight (lines 27–28).

EXERCISE
📖 **Read Genesis 1:1–2. Then return to lines 30–32.**

What do the words 'hatched' and 'quick'ning' suggest to you and how are they related to the traditional iconography (artistic representation) of the Holy Spirit? ▶▶

> Discuss the importance of these lines for the whole poem's pre-occupation with the promise and renewal of life.

This exercise will have reminded you that human beings on their own would never arrive at understandings like these. Only through the illumination of the Holy Spirit will the mind make such a leap (John 16:13). This is also the Spirit who is present at creation, '*brooding* on the face of the waters' like a bird (one reason for depicting the Spirit as a dove) and to make that association is to acknowledge in another way the continuously creating presence and sustaining purpose of God.

Beyond present experience

Lines 33–36 return to a more sober and reflective tone, after the ecstatic cry of recognition and understanding in lines 23–32. Again, we find the speaker meditating on the characteristics of the waterfall. But this time, he seems more concerned with the signs of death than with the signs of life. Once the water has fallen into the pool below, a pattern of rings forms slowly on the surface, turning dramatic motion almost into stillness again as it 'restagnates all'. You will have seen this phenomenon either in a waterfall or when you have thrown a stone into a pool. The rings that form gradually spread out, fade and disappear towards the edge. The speaker sees this as an image of the ending of human life, for 'just so pass men'. We are powerfully reminded of the plea at the end of Psalm 39, a psalm that has been part of the Anglican funeral service since the seventeenth century:

> For I am a stranger with thee: and a sojourner, as all my fathers were.
> O spare me a little, that I may recover my strength: before I
> go hence, and be no more seen. (Psalm 39:13–14)

This petition is rooted in the Jewish understanding of physical death as an ending, after which souls went to a shadowy place called Sheol, where they would no longer have any possibility of communication with God. But that is not the end of the story that 'The Waterfall' recounts. Human life, divinely created, has an inheritance that cannot be measured in any earthly terms. It is 'an invisible estate', the promise of eternal life through the death and resurrection of Jesus Christ.

EXERCISE

📖 Read Romans 8:1–25, concentrating especially on verse 21.

The chapter affirms that confidence in the Spirit gives us the right to hope for the 'glorious liberty of the children of God'. Think about the difference this promise makes to the speaker's interpretation of the disappearing rings in the pool beneath the waterfall.

For the speaker, this realisation demands a radical readjustment of focus and purpose. Instead of fearing the ending of the earthly 'channel', he must rejoice in the possibility of a smooth course, freed from the burdens and difficulties of earthly life, imaged in the rocky 'cataracts and creeks' of the waterfall.

Final reflection

You may at first have been reluctant to accept that a period of quiet contemplation beside a waterfall could lead to a meditation on life, death and the promise of eternal life. On reflection, however, you may recall times when you have looked at a feature of the landscape for some time and found it leading you into a form of meditation. This may not have been a meditation on a spiritual theme, at least as it would be understood in a Christian framework. It may have been a progression towards deeper self-understanding, or a profounder grasp of your relationship with the world and with other people.

What distinguishes the poem's re-telling of such an experience is the crafting of immediate experience – here, watching the water fall into the pool from a height – into a shape that reproduces that experience in word and picture. In the next poem, you will have the opportunity to see another personal meditation developing, this time beginning with an abstract notion rather than a place or feature. Be alert to similarities and differences between the two poems.

📖 Read George Herbert's *The Bunch of Grapes*:

> Joy, I did lock thee up: but some bad man
>   Hath let thee out again:
> And now, methinks, I am where I began
>   Sev'n years ago: one vogue and vein,

One air of thoughts usurps my brain.
I did towards Canaan draw; but now I am
Brought back to the Red Sea, the sea of shame.

For as the Jews of old by God's command
    Travelled, and saw no town;
So now each Christian hath his journeys spanned:
    Their story pens and sets us down.
    A single deed is small renown.
God's works are wide, and let in future times;
His ancient justice overflows our crimes.

Then have we too our guardian fires and clouds;
    Our Scripture-dew drops fast:
We have our sands and serpents, tents and shrouds;
    Alas! our murmurings come not last.
    But where's the cluster? where's the taste
Of mine inheritance? Lord, if I must borrow,
Let me as well take up their joy, as sorrow.

But can he want the grape, who hath the wine?
    I have their fruit and more.
Blessed be God, who prospered Noah's vine,
    And made it bring forth grapes good store.
    But much more him I must adore,
Who of the Law's sour juice sweet wine did make,
Ev'n God himself being pressèd for my sake.

Back to square one

In 'The Bunch of Grapes', an individual voice describes the despair of
spiritual backsliding and discontent. The image used is that of the wandering of the Israelites in the wilderness, as they journeyed from Egypt
to the Promised Land of Canaan.

EXERCISE
  📖 **Read Exodus 13 to 17.**

Have you experienced a period of spiritual progress, followed by a
sense of regression and spiritual barrenness? Try to recall how long
this lasted, and how it was resolved. ▶▶

In the light of your own experience, can you enter imaginatively into the Israelites' feelings of disillusionment and their sense that God had led them out of Egypt and then left them in the lurch?

The speaker begins by telling the story of the past seven years of his life. He had painstakingly hoarded up a stock of joy, only to find that 'some bad man' had released it. This, of course, raises immediate questions. Joy is a gift that we are encouraged to share with others. It is even debatable whether it has much meaning as a jealously guarded private possession. That leads us to ask whether the man who let joy out really was bad, but final judgement must wait until we have considered the poem in its entirety.

As a result of the loss of happiness, the speaker feels that he has returned to an earlier state of unhappiness. Having come within sight of Canaan, he is pushed back to the Red Sea.

EXERCISE

How would you relate the Promised Land of Canaan and the Red Sea dividing the children of Israel from their slavemasters in Egypt to the experience that is presented in the poem? Note particular reasons for seeing them as effective symbols of achievement and failure in the spiritual life.

Pay special attention to the description of the Red Sea as 'the sea of shame'. You will be able to think of literal reasons for this image, but give some thought also to traditional associations attached to the colour red.

Hope from the tradition

In the second stanza, it seems that the speaker is moving towards some acceptance of his situation. He places his despondency – a typical event in the journey of 'each Christian' – alongside the experience of the Jews who 'travelled and saw no town'. In a sense the Christian life is framed by that story. What all pilgrims on the Christian journey have to understand is that they are participants in a much larger story: they inherit the promises of salvation that begin with God's covenant with Abraham

(Genesis 17); they look forward to the inheritance of eternal life that is promised in Jesus.

To make that point clearer, the speaker draws more comparisons. Like the Israelites in the desert, Christians also have 'guardian fires and clouds' (Exodus 13:21) to mark the guiding presence of God along their way. The Scriptures feed their spiritual hunger, just as the manna from heaven satisfied the physical hunger of the wanderers (Exodus 16:14–15). On the darker side, they have sands and serpents (Numbers 21:8). They are not immune, either, from the dissatisfactions which the Israelites hurled at God when it seemed that their journey would never end (Exodus 16:2–12).

EXERCISE

Make a list of the elements of Christian life and experience that could be embraced by the biblical metaphors discussed in the paragraph above.

Among other things, the previous exercise might have reminded you of the promise of the Holy Spirit, the Comforter (John 14:16; 15:26), sometimes symbolised by fire (Acts 2:3). Perhaps you thought of the new covenant of grace that replaces the old covenant of Law, just as the wine is distilled out of the grape. At the end of the catalogue of similarities, however, the speaker cries out against an inconsistency in the two parallel stories. When the Jews were nearing the Promised Land, they sent scouts ahead to spy out the countryside. These men returned with pomegranates, figs and a bunch of grapes so large that it had to be carried by two men (Numbers 13:17–25). The people took the fruit as evidence of the richness and fertility of the land God was to give them. But in the Christian life that the poem describes, there seems to be no corresponding event. The speaker empathises with the sorrow of the homeless nation, but cannot find the joy of reaching the end of the journey, figuratively expressed in the delight of biting into a ripe grape and releasing the juice. The poem has thus built up towards what might be called an impasse, an obstacle which cannot be negotiated and threatens to put a stop to any further progress.

Completing the picture

It is at this moment of suspense that a simple but life-changing insight breaks into the speaker's dilemma. For he realises that Christians inherit not only the promise of salvation through the Messiah, but also the fulfilment of that promise. He makes the contrast, therefore, between the old covenant and the new. God kept faith with the patriarchs and 'prospered Noah's vine' (Genesis 9:20). But Jesus Christ brings in the new covenant that 'of the Law's sour juice sweet wine did make'.

EXERCISE

📖 **Read Galatians 3.** This passage discusses the movement from the reign of the law under the old covenant and its displacement by faith in Christ.

Spend some time considering the difference between a straightforward abolition of an old system and the addition of new benefits after due preparation under the old system.

The poem's final image and its title are appropriately viewed together. The speaker thinks of the harshness of the law in terms of sour, unfermented juice, unfinished by the careful work of the winemaker. There is certainly promise in the juice, but immense patience is required before that promise comes to fruition. The coming of Christ, the true vine (John 15:1), who tells his disciples that he comes not to destroy the law but to fulfil it (Matthew 5:17), is likened to the process of maturation. The bunch of grapes of the title is therefore a rich metaphor of promise: the promise of God's faithfulness to his wandering people and the promise of salvation through his Son, who is also the shoot from the stock of Jesse (Isaiah 11:1) and thus a lineal descendant of earlier participants in a covenant with God.

Just as Christ does not destroy the old law, however, the new wine does not totally obliterate the acidity of the juice from which it is made. This gives rise to the almost grotesque closing metaphor. As the bunch of grapes is trodden in the winepress to produce the juice, so Christ's body was pierced on the cross to release his blood for our salvation.

How far can you go?

In the last lines of the poem, we come to a personal, intimate understanding of salvation that is part of a development rooted in the promises of the Old Testament. God kept faith with Noah in the 'sour juice' of the old law. Christ completes the process by transforming the old covenant into the new covenant of grace and forgiveness through his death. Here, we are invited to reflect on the gratitude that is expressed every time the Eucharist is celebrated and the blood of the new covenant is symbolically shared.

Nevertheless, to compare the winemaking process with the crucifixion is a daring move. You may have hesitated at that point and wondered whether it was too daring. If the comparison affected you strongly, even if it seemed shocking, then it succeeded in shaping a new perception. What we discover in a poem like 'The Bunch of Grapes' is that the language of passionate belief can be as confrontational as the language of despair or disbelief that we have already encountered in Hopkins and Larkin. The risk of reading under confrontational conditions is that we ourselves may be reshaped.

Further reading

Useful editions
Martz, L L (ed.) (1986), *George Herbert and Henry Vaughan*, Oxford and New York, Oxford University Press.
Patrides, C A (ed.) (1974), *The English Poems of George Herbert*, London, Everyman.

Background
Dyas, D (1997), *Images of Faith in English Literature 700-1500*, London, Longman. (This is a useful guide to Christian symbols used in literature and still helpful for seventeenth-century poetry.)
Freeman, R (1948), *English Emblem Books*, London, Chatto and Windus. (This treats English emblem books, which gave rise to pattern poems like 'The Waterfall'.)

Criticism
Bennett, J (1963), *Five Metaphysical Poets*, Cambridge, Cambridge University Press.
Martz, L L (1962), *The Poetry of Meditation*, New Haven, Connecticut, Yale University Press (second edition).
Martz, L L (1964), *The Paradise Within: studies in Vaughan, Traherne, and Milton*, New Haven, Connecticut and London, Yale University Press.

Post, J (1982), *Henry Vaughan: the unfolding vision*, Princeton, New Jersey, Princeton University Press.

Tuve, R (1952), *A Reading of George Herbert*, London, Faber and Faber.

Vendler, H (1975), *The Poetry of George Herbert*, Cambridge, Massachusetts and London, Harvard University Press.

7. PATTERNS OF CHRIST

Introduction

In this chapter we see, through readings of two of Oscar Wilde's fairy tales, how the Christlike example that is encountered in Scripture through the teaching of the gospels can be patterned in the telling of other kinds of stories. Through the development and interaction of their characters, the stories show us several approaches to the virtues that are taught and embodied by Jesus as we meet him in the gospels. The shape that Wilde chose for his children's stories builds on themes of generosity, sacrifice and transformation.

All of these themes are key theological preoccupations, and if we have met them through biblical reading we are likely to recognise them at once in other situations. Reciprocally, seeing these themes recast in the patterns of narrative equips us to return to biblical texts with expanded vision. It should never be forgotten, though, that we are engaging with literary creativity as well as a form of instruction or a model for living. This means that there will be many important features that the stories share with biblical examples, but the two forms are not interchangeable.

Reflecting on experience

You will probably be familiar with the genre of fairy tale from your childhood. As you read these stories, think about what they have in common with tales like 'Hansel and Gretel', 'The Snow Queen' or 'Beauty and the Beast'.

In particular, concentrate on signs and messages in stories you have encountered previously. What techniques are used ▶▶

---

in such stories to mark good or evil characters? How are characters rewarded or punished for their actions?

Now give some thought to your reading of the parables of Jesus in the gospels. Do you see any similarities between their method of storytelling and that of the secular narratives you may have read elsewhere?

Typology

The technique of adumbrating (foreshadowing or throwing into relief) qualities and characteristics, or making links and connections between themes and persons, is known as *typology*. We meet it in the Bible in various guises. First of all, there is a *typological* relationship between the Old and New Testaments. A number of New Testament events have Old Testament counterparts. For example Moses' raising of the brass serpent in the wilderness foreshadows the raising of Jesus on the cross (Numbers 21; John 3:14). Jonah's miraculous escape from the belly of the whale is a *type* of the resurrection. The sacrifice of Isaac (Genesis 22) is another type of the sacrifice of the Son of God in the crucifixion.

A second aspect of typology is the identification of people or events as types of a special role, place or function. Thus Moses is the type of the prophet, David is the type of kingship, and Aaron is the type of priesthood. Jerusalem is a type of the place where salvation will be enacted, both within human history in the Old Testament and at the end of time in the New Testament (Revelation 21). The saving of Noah's family in the ark (Genesis 7–8), the Israelites' safe crossing of the Red Sea (Exodus 14) and the healing of Naaman the leper (2 Kings 5) are all types of baptism in the Christian tradition.

A third aspect of typology, and one which will concern us most here, deals with the relationship between patterns and characters in non-biblical narrative and the biblical resonances they call to mind.

Looking for Christ in 'The Happy Prince'

📖 **Read 'The Happy Prince'.**

In this story, a distinctive typology is built up largely around clearly contrasting sets of values. These are some of the obvious polarities, but you will be able to detect more:

- the selfish materialism of the city fathers stands in opposition to the statue's compassion;
- the wealth of the palace is remote from the poverty of many of the city's inhabitants;
- short-sighted preoccupation with one's personal situation comes to be contrasted with a far-reaching concern for human need.

The progress of the tale asks readers to recognise that a process of evaluation is taking place. For that reason, even though you might immediately recognise familiar marks of biblical or Christian teaching, your final conclusions should involve careful attention to the way in which a model is being constructed, or a lesson communicated.

For example, the first few paragraphs of this story adopt a form of *irony* (you have met this device in Larkin's 'Aubade') to show that the Happy Prince is not happy at all. As he tells the Swallow, he confused pleasure with happiness while he was alive. Within the walls of the Palace of Sans-Souci (literally, Carefree Palace), his only experience was of entertainment, companionship and luxury. Only after his death and commemoration in the form of a statue with the properties of speech, sight and emotion – as is possible in fairy tales – is he able to see the misery in his city.

EXERCISE

Spend a few minutes thinking about the consequences for the development of the story, of the Prince's inability to respond practically to the misery he observes. You may find it useful to reflect on the *paradox* of a truly compassionate heart in a statue's lifeless body.

The appearance of the Swallow facilitates acts of kindness that the Prince would otherwise be unable to perform. In the course of the story, their relationship undergoes significant changes. At first, the Swallow offers his services rather grudgingly, agreeing to delay his journey to Egypt by one night in order to deliver the ruby from the Prince's sword to a poor seamstress with a sick child. Later on, although the Swallow still talks of going on to Egypt, his tone has changed. He co-operates willingly in two further acts of mercy, taking the Prince's sapphire eyes to a poor young playwright and a little match girl who has not earned all her father expected during the day.

Notice the reactions of the recipients on each occasion. The play-wright thinks an admirer has rescued him, while the little girl does not realise that the precious stone is anything more than a pretty piece of glass.

Transformation or conversion

It is at this point that the Swallow, having been converted from grudg-ing to voluntary engagement in helping the poor of the city, decides to stay with the now blind Prince for ever. At first, the Swallow keeps up a flow of stories of exotic places, but the Prince soon asks for news of the condition of people in his city. Hearing the reports of poverty and hunger, he instructs the Swallow to strip off his gold leaf covering and distribute it to the poor.

Reflection on the changes in the Prince and the Swallow invites us to think about patterns of *transformation* or even *conversion*. Some of this is self-evident: a shallow human being becomes a statue with a heart, and a selfish, frivolous bird finds itself drawn into the costly conse-quences of loyal friendship. But we must take our questions further.

EXERCISE
Transformation in this story is a process or a pattern of growth. How should we measure the changes in the Swallow? While he co-operates in the Prince's acts of generosity, does the story make it clear that he is personally committed to the relief of the poor?

By the same token, how should we interpret the Prince's failure to understand that the Swallow's 'Goodbye' means death, not depar-ture to Egypt?

In the course of considering the questions in the exercise above, you will have found little evidence of real self-knowledge in either of the characters. The Prince has learnt about conditions outside the confines of the palace and also about the ingratitude of those who receive gifts. The Swallow has learnt about a love that is more profound than love of self. But the Prince cannot grasp that his companion has given up his life to stay with him, any more than the Swallow can conceive of an independent wish to alleviate suffering.

In the Swallow's case, the story deals elegantly and rather humorously with tensions and changes. Early on, it describes his growing disenchantment with the slender-waisted Reed, who 'has no conversation' and 'is always flirting with the wind'. Later, the Prince asks him to take a ruby to a struggling seamstress with a sick son. The Swallow remarks that he does not like boys, although he ungraciously performs the mission.

God intervenes: a late entry

In neither case are we fully prepared for the final events. The entry of God, who promises Paradise to the Prince and the Swallow, is reminiscent of Jesus' promise to the dying thief on the cross: 'Today you will be with me in Paradise.' Yet the thief's conversion through recognising and acknowledging Jesus, and repenting of his sins, is altogether more rigorous than anything we observe here.

In the end, you may feel that there are arguments in favour of accounting for the events of 'The Happy Prince' without reference to a Christian world-view at all. In assessing this critical question, you should give some thought to interpretations of the co-existence and experience of human beings that omit God from the process. These arguments might include an inherent capacity for generosity and self-giving that has nothing to do with an outside agency.

EXERCISE

Deciding whether God is necessary to, or responsible for, the good impulses and even the spirit of repentance that motivate the Prince will determine what you make of the appearance of God in the two closing paragraphs. Describe the effect that your reading of the closing moments has on your reading of the story as a whole.

The story in the light of Christian tradition

The unsatisfactory conclusion to 'The Happy Prince' must be viewed alongside the fact that the story is marked by a concern to defend the ultimate value of Christian virtue. Some sources and parallels are set out below, and you may wish to add to them.

The gospels present us with many instructions about giving to the poor, caring for the sick and feeding the hungry.

📖 **Look at the examples of this teaching in Matthew 5:4–8 48; Matthew 6:1–4; 19–23; Luke 6:31–36 and Luke 12:32–34.**

Just as Scripture sets a pattern of care, it also provides images of the failure of care.

📖 **Read the story of the wicked steward (Matthew 18:23–35).** This illustrates God's displeasure at ungenerous and ungrateful behaviour. Jesus was fierce in his condemnation of those with official status who neglected the poor (Mark 12:38–40).

We are also warned against laying up treasures on earth: our real treasure is a lasting one to be laid up in heaven.

📖 **Read Matthew 6:19–20; Mark 10:17–22 and Luke 12:16–21.**

Self-renunciation, we learn from Mark 8:34–37, is a condition of following Christ. Jesus tells his disciples that the commandment, second only in importance to a love of God, that involves every aspect of our beings is to love our neighbour as ourselves (Mark 12:28–34). The extent of the demand that such a love can make is spelt out in John 15:13, which proclaims that there is no love greater than laying down one's life for one's friends.

What do we learn from the unresolved questions?

The first chapter reminded readers that there is no simple fit between biblical teaching and works of literature with Christian themes and traces. We might have wished we could say that the Prince was a 'type' of Christ, or that the Swallow was a type of the penitent thief who acknowledged Jesus and asked for a place in his Kingdom as they hung side by side on their crosses. But the story will not allow us to do that.

In a similar way, we might have expected a difference in at least some of the lives that were changed by the Prince's gifts. Why are there only material transformations and no spiritual transformations? Are the city fathers in certain ways the most plausible and consistent characters?

EXERCISE
Go back to 'The Happy Prince' and identify the events or reactions in the story that point directly to Christian or biblical parallels. You may find it helpful to set these out in two columns.

Then spend some time reflecting on any details that make a typological interpretation (in other words, a direct fit between the columns) problematic.

Once you have thought about these issues, read the following critical reflection on Wilde's fairy tales:

> [These stories are] the work of an adult fascinated by the young. Children stand for purity and simplicity . . . They show an instinctive understanding of the forces of nature . . . [They are] essentially parables; but instead of presenting images of the desirable, they emerge, as often as not, as sermons by a sceptic to the relentlessly unconverted. While the Biblical parable is intrinsically didactic and incidentally narrative, Wilde's parables tend to be intrinsically narrative and only incidentally didactic, even though their 'moral' basis, in the general sense of the word, is unmistakable. (Shewan, 1977, p. 38)

Looking for Christ in 'The Selfish Giant'

📖 Read 'The Selfish Giant'.

Like 'The Happy Prince', 'The Selfish Giant' turns on contrasts in human values. More specifically, we might even say that both stories examine selfish worldly values against Christian values. Crucial to the development of the narrative is the opposition between childhood innocence and adult suspicion, loneliness and companionship, and selfishness and sharing. Unlike 'The Happy Prince', 'The Selfish Giant' exploits one key symbolic device to reflect what we might term generally spiritual retardation and growth. This, of course, is the garden.

EXERCISE

Trace the changes that occur in the garden in the course of the story, and try to link them to the interaction that takes place between characters. In particular, make a note of your thoughts about the blossoming tree, too tall for the little boy to climb without the Giant's assistance.

'The Selfish Giant' as parable of Christ

Whereas 'The Happy Prince' gives strong hints of Christlike values and actions, without actually producing a Christ-figure, 'The Selfish Giant' is explicitly a tale of Christ present in the world. There is no difficulty in identifying the little boy, who returns at the end of the story to reveal his wounded hands, as a Christ-figure. More important, perhaps, is the task of tracing the way that the story unfolds towards this revelation. This cannot be divorced from the Giant's growth from selfishness to generosity, and from sour behaviour to love. But here stands another paradox. Everything the tradition tells us about privileged encounters with Christ includes a gain in knowledge along with a reformation of character. Yet the Giant is quite unaware of the child's identity and its meaning, even when he is being summoned to his death.

Rodney Shewan is able to show that the Giant comes at best to a rudimentary understanding of the link between the child's wounds and the blossoming tree. This is what he has to say:

> By comparison with the Happy Prince's penance, the Giant's is a mere token; and although he re-establishes contact with the mysterious forces of nature by placing the child in the tree, he neither knows the symbolic significance of his action, nor even that the Crucifixion has taken place. Yet the bare tree is a traditional symbol for the rood [i.e. the Cross], and the Giant's action unwittingly confirms that pain and sorrow necessarily precede redemption. The 'wounds of love' cause the white flowers of love to spring, and, once the Giant understands this, his corpse is strewn with them by the elemental powers. (Shewan, 1977, pp. 42–43)

> **EXERCISE**
>
> Does the story give its readers any preparation for the child's expla-
> nation of his wounds: 'but these are the wounds of love', or any
> assistance in interpreting them?
>
> Does it give adequate weight and conviction to the Giant's conver-
> sion?

The story in the light of Christian tradition

After the resurrection, Jesus appears to his followers on several occasions. Luke's account of the journey to Emmaus (24:13–32) tells how
two of the apostles travelled and conversed with the risen Christ for
some time without recognising him. Only when he broke bread at a
meal did they know who he was. Jesus reappears in Jerusalem, where his
companions on the Emmaus road meet him again. This time, he points
to his hands and his feet as identifying features (Luke 24:36–40). The
Apostle Thomas acknowledges Jesus as 'My Lord and my God' when
Jesus invites him to put his hand into the wound in his side (John
20:25–28). On all of these occasions, the marks mean something to the
witnesses. For later generations of Christians the five wounds have
become symbolic of the crucified Christ.

Does this evidence entitle us to judge the significance of the Giant's
experience of the Christ he does not recognise? In making an evaluation, we should remember Jesus' teaching on the importance of receiv-
ing children lovingly, and never harming or corrupting them.

📖 **Remind yourself of Matthew 19:13–15; Mark 9:33–37, 42 and
Mark 10:13–17.** The Letter to the Hebrews (13:2) reminds its audience that by showing kindness to strangeness, some have 'enter-
tained angels unawares'. More complex, but not irrelevant, are the
risen Jesus' words to Thomas, who recognises him by his wounds:
'Blessed are they that have not seen, and yet have believed' (John
20:29).

More generally, gardens and trees are frequently encountered symbols in the Old and New Testaments. They carry a range of significance,
and you should not expect the Garden of Eden in Genesis to be
deployed in exactly the same way as the gardens that the prophets use to

characterise the relationship between the inhabitants of the land and God. Again, the Song of Songs uses the garden as an erotic symbol.

There is an ancient association between the tree that brought sin and mortality into the Garden of Eden and the cross, the tree of life. Medieval interpreters believed that the site of the crucifixion was identical with the site of Adam's tomb, and this of course emphasises the reciprocity between Christ's atoning death and Adam's sin, summed up by St Paul in 1 Corinthians 15:21–22. A medieval lyric puts the association like this: 'Man stole the fruit, but I must climb the tree.' Artistic representations of the crucifixion frequently show blood and water pouring out of Christ's side into the mouth of Adam's skull below.

EXERCISE

You may feel that 'The Selfish Giant' is a simpler story than 'The Happy Prince'. If you have the opportunity to share your reflections with other students, discuss the reasons for this.

You will find it helpful to look at the relationships between different characters; the changes in the Giant's behaviour; and the clues that lead to the last meeting between the Giant and the little boy shortly before the Giant's death.

Reflections in the light of the Christian evidence

We can certainly make something out of the delightful parallel between the Giant's garden where the little boy played, and the garden of Paradise which is where he will take the Giant. Yet the Giant's transformation, mirrored in the changes in his garden, does not provide a straightforward account of a change of heart that leads to salvation. In fact, it teaches us no more about death than that a repentant and loving state of mind is good preparation for dying. This means that the reader has to do a great deal of work to interpret the tale as a parable of earthly life as the school of heaven.

More disquietingly, the child's wounds introduce a 'grown-up' question about sacrifice in a story that can only supply help at a childlike level. Before trying to form a conclusion about this difficulty, you should give some thought to the checklist below.

• Both 'The Happy Prince' and 'The Selfish Giant' employ a number of

fairy tale elements, though they include conventional human characters. You might try to identify the fairy tale features and write down your reactions to their place in the narratives.
- The style of language used in a literary work is never arbitrarily chosen. These stories use simple sentences, but also rely on a rather old-fashioned style of language. Is this suitable for their subject-matter?
- Do you find a disjunction or mismatch between differing levels of sophistication within each story? For example, you might focus on the Swallow's passing romance with the Reed and the reasons for his growing boredom, or the Giant's decision to return from his seven-year visit to the Cornish Ogre.
- How does the setting of the stories in both a real and a fairy tale world, where statues talk to birds and giants live in the suburbs, affect your response?
- Can these stories be seriously considered as *children's* stories?
- Do you think that the difficult questions raised in both stories are resolved?

When questions remain unanswered

As you have worked through the list above, you will have become more and more aware that 'The Selfish Giant' raises a number of issues that cannot be closed simply by suggesting that the Giant will complete his transformation by going to heaven. There are plenty of clues that invite us to see this as a strong possibility, but nothing to explain why the little boy had to suffer, or how the Giant discovered that there was something more profound than a blossoming garden to be grasped in his friendship with the children.

It has been said that there are many quick, easy answers to difficult questions. Implied in that is the claim that most of them are wrong. The most disconcerting discovery in a reading assignment like this may be that the stories do not always allow us to apply the familiar answers of Christian teaching to the problems that they raise. You should persevere with the questions, however. Sometimes it is more fruitful to live with unresolved issues than to provide superficial solutions.

Further reading

Ellmann, R (1987), *Oscar Wilde*, London, Hamish Hamilton.

Fabiny, T (1992), *The Lion and the Lamb: figuralism and fulfilment in the Bible, art and literature*, London, Macmillan.

Murray, I (ed.) (1989), *Oscar Wilde: a selection*, Oxford, Oxford University Press, Introduction.

Nassaar, C (1974), *Into the Demon Universe*, New Haven, Connecticut, Yale University Press.

8. STORY INTERPRETING STORY

Introduction

Novels, stories, poems and plays repeatedly show how abstract elements of experience, or motivation, or personality can be presented in a concrete and tangible way. It is possible to talk about 'sin', for example, without having any clear idea what exactly the word covers. Telling a story of a brutal murder, on the other hand, immediately grounds the concept in an event involving human beings and the forces that drive their actions. This, in turn, helps us to return to the original concept with clearer understanding.

The distortions in human action that might be gathered under the heading of 'sin' are often illustrated in biblical literature by a series of arresting images: wicked stewards, unfruitful vines and fig trees, fickle wives. Equally, there are many ways of depicting love and generosity in descriptions of God's motherly care, parables of kindness, and images of the marriage between God and the chosen people.

In this chapter, we will examine two literary explorations of human failing: the portrayal of the Seven Deadly Sins in the fourteenth-century poem, *Piers Plowman*, and the embodiment of deceit, greed, selfishness and exploitation in the characters of J B Priestley's play, *An Inspector Calls*. In *Piers Plowman* the representation of the dark side of human nature is balanced by signs of turning away from sinful habits, and this starts us on the way to thinking about human redemption. Using the motif of Christian pilgrimage, the poem allows us to imagine the journey of salvation.

> ### Reflecting on experience
> How often do you use or hear expressions like 'the wages of sin', 'the road to ruin', 'the ladder of success' or 'the   ▶▶

green-eyed monster' (as an image of envy)? Try to think back from these figures of speech to the kind of story where 'sin', 'ruin', 'success' or 'envy' could be places or characters.

Try to recall examples of fictional narratives that play out, and to some extent analyse, real-life situations. A secular example is the tale of Red Riding Hood. A biblical example is the parable of the sower (Matthew 13:3–23; Mark 4:3–20; Luke 8:5–15).

What are the 'facts' embedded in the stories on your list?

Allegory

The technique of telling a story that illustrates a further meaning beyond what is obvious at a first reading, and often teaching a particular lesson, is known as *allegory*. It has been described as:

> a narrative in which the agents and action, and sometimes the setting as well, are conceived so as to make coherent sense on the 'literal', or primary level of signification, and also to signify a second, correlated order of agents, concepts and events. (Abrams, 1999)

Allegory comes in two main forms. First of all, there is historical or political allegory, which uses a known narrative to explore a particular situation and highlight its evils and the interplay of the characters involved in it. A well-known example is John Dryden's poem, *Absalom and Achitophel* (1681). Dryden employs the events described in the Second Book of Samuel (the rebellion of Absalom against his father, King David) to discuss the attempted rebellion of the Duke of Monmouth against his father, King Charles II, in the period between 1678 and 1680. The Old Testament characters mentioned in the poem all represent characters in the later historical narrative, with David standing for Charles II, Absalom for the Duke of Monmouth, and Achitophel for the Earl of Shaftesbury who plotted with him.

The second type of allegory is the allegory of ideas. Here, abstract quantities such as goodness and truth, or malice, lust, envy or conscience are personified, or given human characteristics. Sometimes, as we see in *Piers Plowman*, the personified abstraction is identified by its own name. At other times, the allegory works by a combination of symbolic names and other methods of representing human weaknesses and failures. There are instances of this in *An Inspector Calls*.

Allegory has played a very large role in the composition of Scripture. In the Old Testament, for example, the prophet Hosea tells the story of his unfaithful wife.

📖 **Read Hosea 1 to 3.**

This relationship stands for Israel's desertion of God, and its likely consequences. The parables of Jesus offer a particularly clear model. They use allegory as a device for teaching the values of the Kingdom of God, without actually naming these in their stories. You might refer to the story of the labourers in the vineyard (Matthew 20) as one of many such parables. Here, the events of the story provide a parallel to the issues they allude to, and encourage the readers or hearers to form judgements and learn lessons which can be applied to these issues.

The interpretation of Scripture has also employed allegory. Bernard of Clairvaux (1090–1153) explained the Song of Songs as an evocation of the relationship between Christ and the Church. Likewise, it has played its part in the understanding of the Church's worship. In the middle ages, for example, the mass took on a whole layer of allegorical significance, with each stage being read as an incident in the life of Jesus. You might consider the elements of baptismal symbolism in contemporary experience, and what aspects of the Christian journey they illustrate.

Piers Plowman and the allegory of the Seven Deadly Sins

📖 **Read Book (Passus) V of William Langland's poem, *The Vision of Piers Plowman*.** The poem is written in what we now call Middle English. It becomes easier to read with practice, but initially you are advised to begin with a modern English version. Passus V is a self-contained episode, but readers are encouraged to attempt the whole poem at a later stage.

Langland's fourteenth-century dream-poem is an account of the pilgrimage of the individual soul towards the truth revealed by Christ. It presents this journey dramatically as a series of dream visions experienced by the narrator, whose name – Will – is embedded cryptically in the poem. Critics generally believe that there is a considerable convergence between the author, William Langland (a fourteenth-century cleric) and the narrator who calls himself Long Will. There are setbacks and attractive worldly distractions, often colourfully personified, along the way that unfolds in the dream. The visions end with the founding of Holy Church, presented as a great barn to shelter the faithful against the coming of Antichrist.

Each book of the poem is called a *passus*, a Latin word meaning step. This appropriately suggests the stage-by-stage progress of the journey towards Truth through dreams, and reflections on dreams, and the lessons learned in the process. The events and characters belong recognisably to the times, as their occupations, activities and colloquial speech reveal. But, because this is a story which sets out to teach its readers something about the Christian way, it invites its modern audience to enter fully into its development.

The poem begins on a summer morning on the Malvern Hills in Worcestershire. Here, Will falls asleep and dreams of a tower on a hill, and far below it a dungeon. The tower stands for Truth, the dungeon for Falsehood. A beautiful lady, who identifies herself as Holy Church, tells Will that these two sites are respectively the dwelling places of God and the Devil. So we are introduced to the competition between worldly values and spiritual values, a discussion that goes on through the first four *passus* (the word is the same in the singular and in the plural).

The fifth *passus* of Langland's poem describes a call to repentance, and gives vivid narrative shape to the business of confessing sin and seeking truth. Having woken up briefly, the dreamer falls asleep again and sees Reason, personified as a preacher carrying a cross, addressing a field full of people – the group comprises the king and his subjects. Reason urges them to confess their sins and repent, in a speech which has a strong vein of contemporary reference. He tells them that their sins have been the cause of certain recent natural disasters, notably a violent storm. Scholars have been able to date this event precisely to 1361, thus confirming the close interplay between the world of the poem and the society in which it arises.

Reason targets particular individuals in his audience – the vain, the idle and those in priestly or monastic orders who fail to keep their rule and set an example of godly conduct. He advises them to give up their pilgrimages to popular holy sites like Rome and Compostela, and instead to take up the quest for Truth.

EXERCISE

We usually think of reason as an inner state, and in relation to individuals. So it is strange to find it presented here as an external force addressing people and urging them to action. How would you redescribe the work of Reason in the opening section of Passus V in modern terms?

Enter the Seven Deadly Sins

Langland gives us brief sketches of Pride and Lechery, and elaborate portraits of Envy, Anger, Avarice, Gluttony and Sloth. The longer portraits contain a strong element of the grotesque, exaggerating the most unpleasant characteristics of each of the named figures. You will notice that the characters are situated in the context of the daily life of the times. Envy is a citizen whose relationship with other people is poisoned by hatred and resentment. Anger has worked in a friary garden and a convent kitchen. His main achievement has been to start malicious gossip and cause ill-feeling. Avarice is a dishonest tradesman married to an equally dishonest woman. Gluttony is a gross drunkard, unable to control his excessive behaviour. Sloth is a parish priest who has neglected his ministry and only shown an interest in money.

EXERCISE

Spend some time discussing the descriptions of the Deadly Sins. Take note of their comic elements.

How do the physical characteristics of each portrait help you to gain a clearer sense of the kind of sin to which they belong?

Repentance shows another way

A new character now appears on the scene. This is Repentance, who explains the story of salvation as God's desire to rescue sinners. He points out that it is Mary Magdalene, the woman with a past, to whom Jesus chooses to reveal himself after the resurrection. Next, he invites the sinners on a pilgrimage in search of Truth. In this way, a different kind of allegory is thus introduced: the pilgrimage as Christian journey.

So, from the allegorical presentation of sin as grotesque local characters, we move into a landscape that is richly significant. The pilgrims
will have to cross various obstacles representing the Ten Commandments, but these become the equipment that helps them finally to enter
the Kingdom of Heaven. Still, it is too difficult for some of the strag-
glers, and they fall by the wayside.

The extract we have read comes out of a world in many ways
different from ours, but not an unsophisticated world. For that reason,
you should beware of underestimating the skill of this colourful introduction to the way of salvation. What it shows us is a way of interpreting human existence in relation to God that is deeply interwoven with
biblical teaching.

To appreciate this, you will need to consider the way that a rather
straightforward recommendation to live by the Ten Commandments
and to practise the virtues preached in the gospels becomes part of the
dramatic apparatus of a narrative.

EXERCISE
📖 **Read Exodus 20:1–17.** Then re-read the instructions Piers
gives to the people about the route they must follow to find
truth.

Reflect on the way in which features of the familiar landscape
become a teaching instrument.

Once the pilgrims have passed all the obstacles along the way, Piers
tells them that they will come to a mansion. This, of course, is the home
of Truth, and its architectural elements are all Christian virtues. It is also
an instruction to faith and prayer. The buttresses are 'Believe-or-you-
cannot-be-saved'. The drawbridge is 'Ask-and-you-shall-receive'.
Penance and prayers form the pillars, and the gate hinges are constructed out of almsdeeds, or works of charitable giving.

There are two principal strands to be emphasised in this rich tissue
of biblical allusion. The first is that Jesus is the only way to salvation.
As we read in John 14, he is the way, the truth and the life, and no one
comes to the Father except through him. The second strand takes into
account the response of the believer to God. Both Matthew's and John's
gospels insist that what believers ask for in faith, they will receive

(Matthew 21:22; John 16:24). Luke's gospel is, if anything, more insistent:

> Ask and you will receive; seek and you will find; knock and the door will be opened to you. For everyone who asks receives, those who seek find, and to those who knock, the door will be opened. (Luke 11:9–10, *Revised English Bible*)

But at the end of this quest there is a paradox. For the repentant pilgrims will go through the gate that shut human beings out of Eden after the Fall. (In the medieval tradition Mary's sinlessness reverses the effects of the Fall begun in Eve. This is often represented by the inversion AVE – EVA, where AVE comes from the first line of the *Ave Maria* or Hail Mary, based on Luke 1:28.) Having passed through the gate, the pilgrims discover that Truth is in their own hearts. This is to learn the meaning of Jesus' promise that 'the Kingdom of God is within you' (Luke 17:21). The journey has thus steadily been leading forward to the destination of Truth, but in another sense it has been leading backwards to the revelation that believers should have understood at the outset.

An Inspector Calls: the consequences of the past

📖 Read *An Inspector Calls*, by J B Priestley. If possible read it in full, but concentrate particularly on Acts I and III.

First published in 1947, *An Inspector Calls* is set in a world much closer to ours in time than the world of *Piers Plowman*, but in many senses almost as far away. The action takes place in 1912, in an industrial town in the north of England. The First World War has yet to happen and the Titanic is still in the shipbuilders' yard. Society is rigidly divided by class and Mr Birling, in whose household the play takes place, has clearly moved upwards through his commercial successes and civic activities. This is the background to our first meeting with the Birling family, Gerald Croft and the mysterious Inspector Goole. Eva Smith/Daisy Renton is physically absent, yet she is made vividly present through her independent association with each of the other characters.

In the last reading exercise, you were introduced to the allegorical technique of discussing abstract entities (for example sins and virtues) as though they were developed personalities. Significant names have a different function in this play, since they are applied only to the characters who hold the action together.

EXERCISE

Before you continue, make a list of the associations that the following names call to mind: Eva; Smith; Renton; Goole. Do not be distracted by spelling.

You will probably have thought of all or some of the following:
- **Eva** calls to mind Eve, the archetypal woman who begins her life completely innocent and falls victim to temptation;
- **Smith** suggests everywoman, or everyman, a universal human being;
- **Renton** unavoidably conjures up images of rental and hire, and reinforces the chilly reality of Eva/Daisy's slide into prostitution once she leaves Milward's Department Store;
- **Goole** is a homophone (that is, a word that sounds identical to another word) of 'ghoul', meaning a ghost or spectre. It is, of course, also a northern place name, and thus reminds us of the play's provincial setting in the north of England, rather than in London.

EXERCISE

Now that you have a sketch of the play's most obviously allegorical features, think again about your responses to the action. Does it succeed in convincing you that its characters are credible people, or do you feel that character and action are simply vehicles for teaching a lesson?

One of the remarkable features of *An Inspector Calls* is that, however one chooses to account for the figure of Inspector Goole, his appearance prefigures an event that is still to happen, rather than a present or past state. But the prefigurement depends on certain past events coming to light as the plot unfolds.

His interviews with the Birlings and Gerald Croft have two immediately striking effects, followed by a third development.
- First of all, they impel each person to confess to a particular encounter or relationship with Eva Smith/Daisy Renton.
- Second, they draw characters into passing judgement on one another's actions. Thus Mr Birling's children convict him of an exploitative attitude to his employees; Sheila proves to have taken advantage of her

parents' privileged position in Brumley; both Gerald and Eric justify their sexual exploitation of Daisy as part of their kind but casual efforts to help her; and Mrs Birling's snobbery and her scorn for the women who come to her agency for help emerge once she begins to describe Daisy's visit.

- The third stage is the re-negotiation of the characters' relationships with one another. Sheila and Gerald stand revealed to each other in such an unpleasant light that their recently announced engagement cannot continue. Mr Birling, who begins the evening confiding that he expects a knighthood (jokingly adding the proviso that this will depend on good behaviour) emerges as someone unworthy of public recognition. Eric has lost the respect and trust of his family. Reciprocally, his parents' callous attitude to the fact that Daisy's suicide has also robbed them of a grandchild is enormously painful to him.

What we learn is that there can be no going back. Too much hurtful information has been brought into the open, so that even if Eva/Daisy had not died, the characters' initial comfortable assumptions about family and society would have been permanently disrupted. All of them have learned contempt for one another and for the assumptions by which they live. Some of them have undergone a kind of moral growth. None of them is at a stage where the close and trusting associations that existed before Inspector Goole's visit can be restored.

EXERCISE

In the light of what has just been discussed, think again about Sheila's comments at two points near to the end of Act III.

On the first occasion, after Mr Birling has triumphantly confirmed that there is no Inspector Goole in the Brumley Police Force, she says, 'I suppose we're all nice people now' (p. 213, Penguin edition). On the second occasion, after a call to the Infirmary reveals that no young woman has died of an overdose of disinfectant, she says, 'So nothing really happened. So there's nothing to be sorry for, nothing to learn. We can all go on behaving just as we did' (p. 220, Penguin edition).

The allegory of history

The play brings its audience into unavoidable confrontation with a particular moment in history. You have already been reminded of its setting, at a time just before the First World War when it still seemed possible to hold as certainties many notions that were challenged and rendered obsolete by the catastrophic events that followed. Among the issues that are brought to the fore, we will concentrate on the class system (in many ways the key that unlocks all of the play's tortured complexities), assumptions of privilege and position, and the changing position of women in the family and in society.

The setting of action, in a northern manufacturing town called Brumley, makes an immediate point. This is not fashionable London: it is probably an Industrial Revolution town, perhaps near to Manchester, and the leaders of society have achieved prominence and respect through hard work and industry. As Eva/Daisy's dissatisfaction with the wages at Mr Birling's factory indicates, such success was made possible largely through the availability of cheap labour. The distinction between employers and their staff was growing more fragile, however, and further levelling would take place with the outbreak of war.

That Eva Smith feels sufficiently confident to protest about her working conditions is evidence of increasing awareness among working women of their rights. It would be some time after the war that women won the vote, but the seeds were sown long before. In contrast to this, Mrs Birling and Sheila belong to a class which protects women within the family. Eva/Daisy's fate would be unlikely to overtake Sheila. At the same time, such protection includes the assumption that middle-class women do not work and cannot assume adult responsibilities. That Sheila speaks out in Eva/Daisy's defence suggests that she, and women like her, are also facing a coming of age as they begin to confront the differences between their lives and the lives of less privileged women.

Reflecting on the tradition

An Inspector Calls is a devastating critique of a society that values respectability and status without honouring the integrity and human dignity of those unable to secure a position in society by economic means. It is also a searing examination of the relationships of love and trust between members of a family, or friends, when familiar assump-

STORY INTERPRETING STORY 97

tions are stripped away. All these subjects are addressed, on many occasions and under a wide range of circumstances by biblical teaching.

The New Testament strongly condemns double standards adopted by groups who set themselves apart and look down on the practices of others. Luke's gospel provides a powerful account of Jesus' words to a Pharisee who had invited him to dinner. The Pharisee comments that Jesus has not washed his hands before the meal. Jesus replies in scathing terms, pointing out that the Pharisees observe the customs of hospitality, hygiene and almsgiving and yet harbour evil thoughts and prevent the flourishing of other people (Luke 11:37–53).

Payment of just wages to labourers is a tenet of biblical ethics. Leviticus 19:13 and Deuteronomy 24:14–15 emphasise this, and Jesus uses the metaphor of the labourer who is worthy of his hire (Luke 10:7). The parable of the labourers in the vineyard (Matthew 20) insists that contractual agreements should be honoured.

Judging others is an occupation fraught with dangers. Matthew 7:1–5 warns against passing judgement, in case we should ourselves be judged. In the particular case of the woman taken in adultery (John 8:1–11) – an incident that is poignantly relevant to Eva/Daisy's career – Jesus says some trenchant words to the accusers preparing to stone her: 'Let whichever of you is free from sin throw the first stone at her.'

The looming presence of Inspector Goole introduces something like an Old Testament figure of prophecy, placing the other characters face to face with the responsibilities attached to their careless or cynical or frankly selfish actions. More than this, it moves the play from the first-level frame of social commentary into the much larger dimension of apocalyptic. Apocalyptic is a term that can be used to describe a dramatically revelatory and even world-ending moment: a moment after which things can never be the same again, if they continue at all.

You will find it helpful to reflect on Luke 12:17–21. Here, Jesus makes the contrast between the securities of worldly wealth, and that time in every human life when no amount of money will protect us from frightening confrontations. The Birlings and Gerald Croft have indeed had the encounter that requires their souls of them.

Allegory as a lesson for life

In *Piers Plowman* and *An Inspector Calls*, we have examined particular techniques for representing reality. In very different ways, the two works address human weaknesses and failings, and the implications these have for life within human history and for the history of salvation.

At a first level, the subject-matter might appear very far removed from our own experience. The deliberately grotesque personification of the Seven Deadly Sins, or the visit of a police inspector who does not exist to discuss an event which has not happened belong to the realm of fantasy. Another way of viewing the operation of allegory is to see its apparent distance from real life as a virtue. The following passage explains what the allegorical method of representation can help us to see:

> The literary allegory does not oppose a realistic account of the universe. Its very power lies in its giving proof to the physical and ethical realities of life objectively conceived ... The symbolic nature of the literal dimension evokes in the reader the recognition that his own experience parallels the expanding implications of the symbolic material in the narrative. (Honig, 1959, pp. 179–180)

In other words, literary allegory can help us to understand complete patterns of action and experience. That is not to say that such understanding will improve our self-understanding to the extent that we become better people. But it does enable us to stand back from our own lives, and to recognise what we have in common with the patterns described for us, and how we fit into a tradition. It shows us how we might share in the great promises of redemption and salvation, and it shows us just as powerfully how we might lose our stake.

Further reading

Bloomfield, M (1981), *Allegory, Myth and Symbol*, Cambridge, Massachusetts and London, Harvard University Press.

Hardison, O B (1965), *Christian Rite and Christian Drama*, Baltimore, Maryland, Johns Hopkins University Press.

McQueen, J (1970), *Allegory*, London, Methuen.

Priestley, J B (1991), *An Inspector Calls*, ed. J Markus and P Jordan, Harlow, Longman. (This contains helpful notes and exercises.)

Salter, E (1983), *Fourteenth-Century English Poetry: contexts and readings*, Oxford, Clarendon.

Summers, V (1987), *J B Priestley: An Inspector Calls* (Penguin Passnotes Series), Harmondsworth, Penguin.

Whitman, J (1987), *Allegory: the dynamics of an ancient and medieval technique*, Oxford, Clarendon.

9. RE-TELLING GOD'S STORY

Introduction

John Milton's epic poem, *Paradise Lost*, charts the course of the creation and fall of humanity, culminating in the expulsion of Adam and Eve from Eden. It is based largely on the narrative in Genesis 1–4, although it expands its scope to encompass the fall of the angels and the war in heaven between God and the rebel angels described in the Book of Revelation. In this chapter, we will study one episode from the larger history: the moment of the Fall itself, and the events immediately preceding and following it.

📖 **Read Book IX of *Paradise Lost*.** Make sure that you read the short prose summary ('The Argument') that precedes the book itself. This will help you towards a good overview of the story you are about to follow.

📖 **Alongside this, you should read Genesis 1 to 3.**

A re-working is, by its nature, a re-interpretation, and Milton's poem is a very strong re-reading of the biblical tale. It means to some extent taking sides, or at least portraying characters as being capable of certain actions with disastrous consequences. Readers will see, for example, that Eve has to be 'set up' in order to make her susceptibility to the serpent's persuasion plausible. Notice that Milton has adopted the second creation narrative (Genesis 2:4b–24), in which Eve is formed from flesh taken out of Adam's side as he sleeps. This order of creation is used throughout the poem to suggest Eve's subordination to Adam.

Reflecting on experience

Think of an occasion (or occasions) when you have produced a rational case for pursuing a course of action that seemed unwise or downright bad to other people concerned. Try to remember whether you were quite convinced that you were doing the right thing, or whether your reasons revealed your own doubts.

Did the efforts of your loved ones or friends or advisers to dissuade you have any effect? If you continued as you had originally intended, did you regret the consequences?

Setting the scene for the Fall

The opening lines of Book IX signal an urgency, and a change to a darker trend in the story of the first human beings and their relationship with God. Up to this point, the poem has celebrated Adam and Eve's love for each other (Books IV and V), their joy in the garden that has been given to them and their conversation with the Archangel Raphael (Books V and VIII), who explains something of the process of creation. Certainly, the discontented and vengeful presence of Satan and the rest of his band of fallen angels has been felt. Book II describes the council of war in the demon city of Pandemonium, in which the rebels discuss a way of taking action against God. Book VI, moving to a point that is chronologically earlier than this, describes the war in heaven and the resulting fall of the rebel angels. But so far, apart from one occasion when Satan (transformed into a toad) was caught by the archangel Gabriel attempting to whisper in Eve's ear, the human pair have known of the existence of evil, but they have had no experience of it. The events of Book IX dramatically destroy their state of innocence.

To gain a sense of some of the key points in the movement towards the Fall, and of the dramatic re-working that the Genesis account undergoes in Milton's hands, this chapter will ask you to examine a series of passages in some detail. To begin, we consider Eve's wish to work away from Adam for a morning.

> **EXERCISE**
> 📖 **Re-read lines 192–225.**
>
> Identify Eve's chief concerns as she proposes that she and Adam should work separately. Pay particular attention to the description of the plants that grow in the Garden of Eden, noting suggestions of disorder or waywardness.
>
> Also consider the issue of *earning* the 'hour of supper' in Paradise.

After the human pair have made their morning offering of praise to God (lines 197–199), Eve makes what seems a perfectly reasonable suggestion to Adam. She has noticed the need for a new strategy for tending the garden, 'for much their work outgrew/ The hands' dispatch of two gard'ning so wide'. Until they have children who can help them (line 207), the task is formidable and all the time the garden is becoming more and more abundant. The descriptive language hints that its prolific growth is not altogether a good development. Eve worries that:

> What we by day
> Lop overgrown, or prune, or prop or bind,
> One night or two with wanton growth derides,
> Tending to wild.
> (lines 209–211)

There are signs that the garden is getting out of control. Words like 'overgrown' and 'wanton' compete with the vocabulary of discipline. So far, this is no more than a tendency or inclination, but the potential for something more alarming is implicit in what is at this stage a charming natural setting.

Men and women in Paradise Lost

Were you to compare this passage with passages in Book IV describing the newly created couple, you would find an intriguing similarity in the language used to depict Eve. While Adam's hair is orderly, 'She as a veil down to the slender waist/ Her unadornèd golden tresses wore/ Disheveled, but in wanton ringlets/ As the vine curls her tendrils' (Book IV, lines 304–307). As the course of the narrative in Book IX progresses, bear in mind the comparison, and the assumptions that it may eventually encourage readers of the poem to make about Eve's propensity to succumb to temptation.

EXERCISE
📖 **Re-read lines 225–269.**

How does the passage balance Adam's respect for Eve's reasoning powers, his sense of an appropriate role for a wife, and the protective role that he believes husbands ought to exercise? Do you detect any contradiction in the way that all three matters are introduced in these lines?

What differences do you observe between Adam and Eve's view of work and its rewards?

Finally, consider Adam's fear that the enemy that lurks near them may attack one of them if they work separately.

Adam's reply makes it clear that he is most reluctant to let Eve out of his sight. In the course of studying his argument, you will have seen that his motives are complex. Certainly, he is pleased that Eve is applying her intellect to the problem of the garden (lines 229–231). Yet this praise is almost immediately undercut by a statement that limits women to the domestic sphere, working in the background to promote 'good works' in their husbands. This sentiment comes directly from the Book of Proverbs (31:10–31) and, like the remark in lines 267–269, reveals a benevolent but ultimately subordinating view of women.

Before raising objections from within the framework of a modern feminist consciousness, we should remember the differences between seventeenth-century English society and social conditions today. That is not to acquit Milton of a restrictive approach to women's independence and their opportunities for intellectual advancement. But it does recognise that he wrote out of an experience that saw the domestic hierarchy as a stabilising social force. In the later group of lines (lines 267–269), there is an anachronistic reference to biblical texts that insist upon the loving, but superior relationship of the husband to the wife (Ephesians 5:22, 5:25; Colossians 3:18–19; Titus 2:5; 1 Peter 3:1). *Paradise Lost* is not simply *re-telling* a story: among other things, it is *re-interpreting* it in the light of a seventeenth-century understanding of New Testament texts.

Adam's superiority is implied in two further ways. He demonstrates his higher understanding of God's intentions by gently refuting Eve's concern that less effective work will mean less right to God's provision at suppertime. Adam assures her that their creator never intended that Eden be governed by a work ethic. It is all a gift. Even work is given to human beings for enjoyment and they are given to each other for loving companionship while they work. In due course, they will be given children to share the tasks of caring for their created home. So, while he might be able to contemplate a short separation ('for solitude sometimes is best society', line 249), he can see no argument for a formal division of labour.

This leads to another piece of insight into the possible strategy of the nameless enemy who has figured in warnings from the archangels. Adam fears that this being might be motivated either by a wish to separate God from human beings, or to destroy the love that binds human beings to one another. He sees his role as being with Eve to protect her and perhaps even to face hardship with her. Your reading of the whole book will have shown you that this is a piece of ironic prophecy. Adam has no means of imagining, in unfallen Eden, what it might be like to endure 'the worst', and when he is put to the test it is not long before he begins to disclaim all responsibility for the situation they find themselves facing.

Eve's reaction to Adam's anxieties might be described as injured innocence. She suggests that Adam does not trust her to stand firm against the enemy, and although he argues that it is not Eve who is weaker without him, but he who is stronger in her presence, she sees this as a sad commentary on their situation in Eden.

EXERCISE
Spend some time reflecting on the motivation of each speaker in this dialogue. Are their positions representative of what critics have called 'unfallen language'? In other words, do they genuinely feel that they are acting within God's provision for life in Eden? Or are they using apparently reasonable claims to justify their preferences without reference to God? This would constitute 'fallen language'. ▶▶

Lines 271, 279–281, 309–316, 321–326 and 335–340 will be helpful references, although you should not expect to arrive at a clear or simple answer.

Temptation and fall

Against a background of gentle disagreement and righteous indignation, Eve sets out alone. As Adam foresaw, Satan, now using the body of the serpent for his disguise, quickly takes advantage of this opportunity. But before we come to consider the persuasive speech that leads her to break God's only constraint on Eden, we should reflect on the pathos of Satan's own condition. Rebellious and vindictive though he is, he is not immune to the beauty and goodness of the newly created earth and its human inhabitants. 'With what delight could I have walked thee round', he exclaims (line 114). All that stops him is his inability any longer to enjoy the loveliness of created things without envying the God who made them. This is not by any means a simple state of affairs. That he can 'in none of these [attractive features of the landscape] find place or refuge' results from the vicious inner conflict that will eventually lead him to encourage Eve to disobey God. As he says:

> the more I see
> Pleasures about me, so much more I feel
> Torment within me, as from the hateful siege
> Of contraries; all good to me becomes
> Bane, and in heav'n much worse would be my state.
> But neither here seek I, no, nor in heav'n
> To dwell, unless by mast'ring heav'n's Supreme;
> Nor hope to be myself less miserable
> By what I seek, but others to make such
> As I, though thereby worse to me redound.
> For only in destroying I find ease
> To my relentless thoughts;
> (lines 119–130)

A penitent return to God is therefore impossible for Satan, and that predetermines the outcome of his encounter with Eve. For a moment, though, we glimpse the possibility of his redemption as he watches her at work in the garden. Everything about her 'overawed/ His malice' (lines 460–461) and his destructive intentions are temporarily displaced:

> That space the Evil One abstracted stood
> From his own evil, and for the time remained
> Stupidly good, of enmity disarmed,
> Of guile, of hate, of envy, of revenge
> (lines 463–466)

The wish to sabotage Adam and Eve's happiness returns almost at once, and driven by hatred, Satan – or as Eve thinks, the serpent – begins to speak.

EXERCISE
📖 **Read lines 494–531.**

You should consult the notes in your edition of *Paradise Lost*, or a classical dictionary, for the classical and mythological references (lines 505–510).

Give some thought to the reasons for comparing Satan's transformation with similar transformations in Greek and Roman literature. Then make a list of words that suggest a convoluted path rather than a straight course, for example 'indented' (line 466). How do the images of oblique movement contribute to presenting Satan as a 'fraudulent' speaker (line 531)?

In this exercise, you will have seen two devices at work to reinforce the contrast between Satan's guile and Eve's innocence. Pagan references (in this case to mythological stories) are frequently used by Christian writers to place characters or situations outside of a Christian framework, while a variety of metaphors for a trait works to imprint a particular sense of a character upon the mind of the audience. By the time Satan begins to speak, then, his evil is established.

Eve's astonishment at hearing 'Language of man pronounced/ By tongue of brute' (lines 553–554) once more constitutes an opportunity, this time for Satan to explain how the serpent acquired such a novel gift. His account of how he found the tree (lines 568–613) begins ordinarily enough, but soon resorts to a vocabulary that is very much more fallen than unfallen. Words like 'desire' (line 564), 'alluring' (line 588), 'long-ing' and 'envying' (line 593) hint at dissatisfaction with the provisions of Eden, and at an aspiration to heights not intended for the serpent and the other animals.

A second distortion appears in Satan's extravagant compliments to Eve, whom he addresses by royal titles. This is praise in a language that belongs exclusively to God. Eve herself seems aware at an elementary level of its inappropriateness and insincerity.

> Serpent, thy overpraising leaves in doubt
> The virtue of that fruit, in thee first proved.
> (lines 615–616)

It is finally Eve's curiosity, the poem suggests, that prompts her to ask where the tree can be found in the garden. To call her 'our credulous mother' (line 644) is not without ambiguity, and we will return to this and other clues to the inevitability of her fall. But at this stage of the dialogue with Satan she is still unquestioningly obedient to God's com-mand (lines 647–652). Or is she? Again the poem provides a way for the boundary of obedience to be ruptured, for Eve knows that obeying is an act of God-given reason (line 654). Already we have heard a good deal on this subject from Adam. When Eve succumbs after hearing and replying to the serpent's eulogy on the powers of the forbidden tree and its fruit, the signs are that reason has given way to faulty reason, or perhaps to no reason at all. It is noon and she is hungry, and 'her rash hand in evil hour/ Forth reaching to the fruit, she plucked to eat' (lines 780–781).

Calculating the damage

The whole natural order suffers the shock of this great turning point in the narrative of Eden (lines 782–783). As for Eve herself, the dismal changes in humanity are written more into the manner than the act of eating. She eats 'greedily' and 'without restraint' until she reaches a state of drunken elation (lines 791–793). It is then that she begins to consid-er the consequences of her action and, in particular, how Adam will be affected.

EXERCISE

Carefully compare Eve's calculations following her fall (lines 816–833) with Adam's grief-stricken words on her return (lines 888–916).

Concentrate on the differences underpinning each partner's decision to remain with the other. In Adam's case, consider whether his profession of love for Eve is an adequate reason for disobeying God.

Eve's dilemma centres on power. Her thinking reacts first against God's rules for inhabiting the garden and the new title, 'our great Forbidder' (line 815), makes this clear. Next, she turns to what she now perceives to be her inferiority to Adam. The chance to invert the hierarchy by holding greater knowledge is a temptation in itself. She foresees a double advantage in being simultaneously more attractive to Adam and less subject to his power of reason. In the end, though, it is fear and jealousy (emotions we have not yet seen in Eden, except in Satan) that hold her back and make her determined that Adam will share whatever fate lies ahead of her. There is a bitter ring in the last lines of her soliloquy:

> So dear I love him, that with him all deaths
> I could endure, without him live no life.
> (lines 832–833)

This is not self-giving love, but self-protecting love, and it is sharply distinguished from the anguished outburst that comes from Adam when she tells him what she has done. Her fall represents for him the fall of the loveliest thing in creation: there is no sense here that he regards her as inferior or that he holds her responsible for her action. Knowing that her death is a certain result, he is unhesitatingly willing to share it with her.

> Should God create another Eve, and I
> Another rib afford, yet loss of thee
> Would never from my heart; no, no! I feel
> The link of nature draw me: flesh of flesh,
> Bone of my bone thou art, and from thy state
> Mine never shall be parted, bliss or woe.
> (lines 911–916)

Yet this moving declaration of faithful devotion, reminiscent in many ways of a marriage vow, is almost immediately tainted as Adam reviews the process of living out his loyalty to Eve. Once more, God-given reason gives way to a form of opportunistic rationalising. Surely, he thinks, God will not 'destroy/ Us his prime creatures'. Although creation could be repeated, this would make God a laughing stock among the enemy angels. It would make the creator seem arbitrarily vindictive (lines 926–951). All of this weakens Adam's repetition of loyalty to Eve. The 'bond of nature' (line 956) that unites them inseparably has been qualified by a cold assessment of the risks involved in eating the fruit, and despite Eve's salute Adam's decision is not purely a 'glorious trial of exceeding love' (lines 961 and 975).

After the Fall

What follows 'the completing of the mortal sin/ Original' (lines 1003–1004) is not a new evil, but the distortion of an existing good. Both Adam and Eve are overcome by sexual desire and make love until they fall into an exhausted sleep. Now this is neither a condemnation of sex, nor a direct linking of sex to the Fall.

📖 **If possible, read** *Paradise Lost* **Book IV, lines 732–734.** This passage describes the tender sexual relationship between Adam and Eve at the beginning of creation.

Dennis Danielson points out that prelapsarian sex (sex before the Fall) was good. The Fall would not have been bad if its chief result had been sexual pleasure. Rather, it is the surrounding consequences that mark the change in the life of human beings (Danielson, 1989, p. 123). Book IX describes uncontrollable desire that drains the partners and fills their sleep with disturbing dreams. When they wake, their new-found knowledge serves only to make them ashamed of being naked. Their earlier trusting love in one another's presence has disappeared. Worse than that, they know that they will never again be able to face God or the angels confidently.

Finding makeshift covering for their bodies is the first step after this. The next development is an ugly exchange of recriminations. Adam blames Eve for leaving his side; Eve objects that he would have been no more able than she was to detect the voice of treachery speaking through the serpent. She follows this with a contradictory argument, initially asking whether she should have stayed beside Adam like 'a lifeless rib' (line 1154), but then pointing out that Adam should have exercised absolute authority in forbidding her to work alone (lines 1155–1156). Adam, outraged, protests that he would have been wrong to restrict Eve's freedom of will (lines 1174–1175). Harsher than this, however, is his parting shot: he was taken in by Eve's attractions, and this is likely to be the fate of anyone who places too much trust in women and allows them the right of self-determination (lines 1179–1186).

Was Eve framed? The constraints of the biblical model

> **EXERCISE**
> In review, can you identify the signs that make it clear that Eve will fall first and then implicate Adam? Look particularly at the phonetic similarity between her name and the word 'evil' (see for example lines 1067–1072), as well as to images of waywardness or weakness (for example lines 209–212, 322–341, 432, 517, 614).

The purpose of the exercise above is twofold. First of all, it asks you to attend to the clues or devices within the narrative that will eventually make the actions of a particular character plausible. Second, it asks you to consider the relationship of the poem to its biblical source in Genesis. The terse account in those early chapters is elaborated into something rich and complex in *Paradise Lost*. But ultimately, faithful representation demands that the poem should arrive at the same conclusion as we find in the original story: Eve must yield to the serpent's blandishments and Adam must accept the fruit from Eve.

Eve's potential to fall becomes increasingly evident in an active way in Book IX. Already in previous books, her physical characteristics – especially the long, wandering tendrils of her hair – have suggested lack of discipline. She describes to Adam how she first came to an awareness of her existence when she woke, saw her reflection in a lake, and almost fell in love with it (Book IV, lines 449–473). In Book IX we hear her described ominously as the 'fairest *unsupported* flower' in the garden (line 432) and this passive image is joined by active indications. She uses her reasoning powers against Adam and she is 'credulous' (an ambiguous word suggesting both trusting innocence and failure of judgement) when she meets the serpent.

The course of the Fall narrative in Genesis perhaps shows us why all this is necessary to the development in *Paradise Lost*. It imposes two constraints, namely that Eve will cause the destruction of humanity, and that this will not be by any predetermined wish of God, but as a result of disobedience. Because Adam and Eve in the poem have been depicted as rounder characters than their biblical counterparts, there has to be motivation, and so Milton must make it possible for Eve to fall. Running alongside this, there is an effort throughout *Paradise Lost* to distinguish God's foreknowledge of the event from predestination.

The unfortunate consequence of these demands upon the composition of the poem is that Eve does, to some extent, appear to have been 'set up'. In the final books, there is some attempt to restore the balance and to show that Adam is independently culpable. But the entrenched impression of Eve is of a weaker, less reliable, intellectually reticent and possibly vain character. Her only bid for independence leads directly to the Fall, and it would be easy to say that the poem endorses a hierarchy of man over woman that could have prevented this from happening.

To leave a reading of Book IX with that impression, without reference to the rest of the epic, would be irresponsible. There are other instances where the equality of Adam and Eve is explicitly stated. For the purposes of this exercise, however, you have had an opportunity to reflect on the challenges and difficulties of re-writing biblical episodes in new literary forms.

Further reading

Crosman, R (1980), *Reading Paradise Lost*, Bloomington, Indiana and London, Indiana University Press.

Fish, S (1997), *Surprised by Sin*, Basingstoke, Macmillan (second edition).

Leonard, J (1989), Language and knowledge in Paradise Lost, in D Danielson (ed.), *The Cambridge Companion to Milton*, pp. 97–111, Cambridge, Cambridge University Press.

McColley, D K (1983), *Milton's Eve*, Urbana, Chicago and London, University of Illinois Press.

Patterson, A (ed.) (1992), *John Milton*, London and New York, Longman. (Patterson demonstrates recent critical approaches and is therefore useful for showing something of the breadth in Milton criticism.)

Potter, L (1986), *A Preface to Milton*, London, Longman. (Contains clear and patient textual readings which – though none are taken from Book IX of *Paradise Lost* – nevertheless show a helpful methodology for those attempting the poem for the first time.)

10. GROUNDS FOR BELIEF

Introduction

How can we be certain about God's purposes for the world?

📖 **Read Penelope Fitzgerald's short novel, *The Gate of Angels.*** The book raises many of the issues implied in that large question.

The novel concentrates on two dominant and apparently competing – or even opposing – themes: the notion that observation or factual explanation are the only grounds for belief; and the notion that events which seem unexplained, providential or accidental nevertheless have within them a trustworthy core. These themes are worked out variously through the accounts of the scientific work that run through the plot, and through the portrayal of the superficially illogical relationship that develops between Fred Fairly and Daisy Saunders. Viewed together, they suggest an intricate and poignant enquiry into the nature of faith itself.

The characters of *The Gate of Angels* inhabit a world where very little seems to be stable. They are brought together by strange and even arbitrary circumstances. For some of them, the discoveries of modern science have cast doubt on earlier notions of creation and order, so that trusting and uncritical belief in God, or a world-ordering being, has become impossible. Yet against this background, personal experiences of human love and happiness offer almost revelatory affirmations of a providence that points to a benevolent origin.

We might call it God. The novel never makes such an explicit claim.

Reflecting on experience
Do you find it difficult to accept that things you cannot see or explain rationally might nevertheless be true? You may ▶▶

find yourself thinking here of divergent phenomena, for example theories that offer to explain aspects of the world we inhabit or unexpected emotional reactions.

Have you met people whose knowledge of the laws of scientific causation makes it difficult for them to believe in God? Try to recall any discussions you might have had.

Interpreting experience

Set in Cambridge in 1912, with a brief excursion into the seamier side of London in the same period, and closely involving the Cavendish Laboratories and the rapid developments in atomic physics that were taking place at the time, this 1991 novel has a firm historical basis in the history of the University of Cambridge and the growth of the discipline of theoretical physics. St Angelicus and its fellows, on the other hand, borrow elements from some of the small Cambridge colleges and from real characters of the day, but that is only the beginning of their portrayal in the novel. Fred and Daisy, and their ordinary yet extraordinary adventures, belong to another level altogether. Throughout the narrative, in other words, there is a skilful interweaving of factual and imagined worlds.

In that light, it is significant that the story begins with an accident. Chronologically, the opening chapter introduces us first to Fred Fairly, cycling through Cambridge at the end of a wet and windy afternoon. But the bicycle accident on the Guestingley Road is the real starting point for all the subsequent events of the novel. It is worth emphasising this, because much of our discussion will rest on the nature of accidents. Are they simply arbitrary events? Or do they have a purpose? Do they depend on providence? Or do they form part of a logical system that governs the operation of the world and human life in the world? The characters of the novel encounter these questions from widely divergent directions, and try to answer them in correspondingly different ways.

EXERCISE
📖 **Read again chapter 7, 'Who is Daisy?'**

Try to notice the false assumptions that ensue from the time that
Fred regains consciousness and first sees the wedding ring on
Daisy's hand, to the entry of the Wrayburns.

At the same time, be aware of the evidence that gives rise to suc-
cessive misapprehensions. For example, why do the Wrayburns
assume that Daisy is Mrs Fairly?

If you find it strange to open the discussion some way into the novel,
you will find it helpful to think about the way in which the bicycle
collision organises the rest of the narrative. Fred's conviction that he
must marry Daisy, having woken up next to her in the Wrayburns'
spare bed, governs his behaviour on returning to St Angelicus on
the wet, windy evening that the first chapter describes. Equally, his
interest in Daisy prompts Holcombe's strange visit and the letters that
hint at Fred's inability to marry, because he is a fellow of his college
and therefore prohibited from marrying. (Also, Holcombe points out,
he would be expected to marry someone of higher social standing
than that of Daisy.) The mysterious nature of the accident occasions
Dr Matthews' strange ghost story, told as a parallel case of an improbable event with an ultimately coherent explanation. Fred's unhappiness
over the event is closely tied to the essay topic he sets his first year
students: 'to devise a rational system of measuring human happiness'
(p. 154).

Just as the accident arranges the behaviour of the characters, so it
organises the chronology of *The Gate of Angels*. It is the single point of
reference before or after which other events occur, and the focus that
gives meaning to other events.

EXERCISE
Bearing in mind the idea of a central event, try to map the other
events of the novel around it. You might attempt this in the form
of a time-line.
➤➤

> Once you have a plan in front of you, consider how a writer might
> have related the other events to each other, had the accident not
> happened.

At this stage, you have examined some of the relationships in time
and space that the novel draws into its development. That process has
largely meant examining objective evidence, in other words trying to
make sense of what appears to be the case. But the reader is also asked
to pay attention to a variety of events or propositions that do not lend
themselves to being proved or explained. It is the purpose of the next
part of the discussion to show that these events play a crucial role in the
novel's subtle examination of the nature of faith.

Faith in *The Gate of Angels*

Faith is difficult to define. The debate about what faith is, and about its
relationship with reason, has gone on throughout the history of Christianity. It includes the following views:
- faith is an act of will and therefore greater than the intellectual facul-
  ty on its own;
- faith and reason are capable of reaching the same conclusions, though
  by different means;
- the same hypothesis could be proved false by reason, but on the other
  hand it could be proved true by faith.

The Gate of Angels does not address these questions in an overt or
didactic way. Instead, it allows them to appear through the characters'
encounters with one another, and through their efforts to explain the
world they inhabit.

The initial scene-setting alerted you to two systems existing side by
side in the milieu that the narrative describes. One of them is occupied
by human relationships that, at least on first inspection, ought to be conventional and ordinary. These include Fred's love for Daisy, his acquain-
tanceship with Skippey, his family relationships and his collegial
association with Professor Flowerdew and the fellows of St Angelicus.
They also embrace Daisy and her mother, her nurse-patient involvement
with James Elder and her short association with Kelly the journalist. The
Wrayburns' marriage presents another conventional human bond.

The other system is occupied by enquiries into the nature and behaviour of the very smallest components of the physical world. Here again, there is diversity. Professor Flowerdew is an extreme case of someone who believes passionately in working from what can be observed. This explains his deeply suspicious attitude to the proposals of the scientists Rutherford and Thomson, who have developed a model for the invisible structure of the atom.

Careful attention to both of these systems will help you to see the kinds of foundations that the characters – consciously or unconsciously – understand to be supporting their world. We will look at three examples in some detail: Daisy's involvement with James Elder, Professor Flowerdew's unhappiness over developments in atomic physics in Cambridge, and Fred's belief in Daisy.

Daisy's faith

The entire middle section of the narrative (Part Two) is devoted to Daisy. It describes her brief history, and explains how she began to train as a nurse at the Blackfriars Hospital after her mother's death. Her nursing career ends because she has tried to act in the best interests of a patient, the young clerk James Elder, who has attempted suicide. As a direct result of her efforts on Elder's behalf, she meets the journalist Kelly, who insists on accompanying her to Cambridge with the undisguised motive of sexually exploiting her lack of income, employment or family support. At the close of Part Two, as the unappealing Kelly puts his arm round Daisy on Liverpool Street Station, 'fingering her' (p.100), there are few signs that anything other than resignation in the face of circumstances is possible. 'What a pair we make, she thought. He doesn't deserve any better, no more do I' (p.100).

This would be a very bleak picture indeed, were it not for Daisy's rooted belief in the transformability of human existence. It is important that you reflect on this before attempting to locate the story told in Part Two in relation to the larger whole.

EXERCISE

📖 **Re-read chapters 11 to 13 to refresh your memory of Part Two.**

Why does Daisy take the step of approaching a newspaper office with James Elder's story? Why is there no evidence of condemnation or disgust in her behaviour towards Kelly?

Certainly where James Elder is concerned, you will have seen Daisy's determination to make it possible for him to believe in himself by seeing his case reported in the press. She recognises his need to have his action treated as significant and her visit to the offices of the *Blackfriars, Vauxhall and Temple Gazette* is a direct response to this need. With adequate recognition, Daisy believes, Elder's life will be transformed. What she discovers when she returns to the hospital, is that his life has simply resumed its old pattern with the woman called Floreen Harris, who has him discharged (p. 96).

Daisy has become unimportant in the whole process. Later, she explains the case matter-of-factly to Fred when they go for a walk in the countryside outside of Cambridge.

> 'Why did you leave London, then? Did you get tired of it?'
> 'I wouldn't ever get tired of it', she said. 'But there's a rule, you know, that you mustn't discuss the patients' cases, not outside the hospital, that is.'
> 'And you did?'
> 'Yes, I did.'
> 'Why, Daisy?'
> 'I thought I'd help him to get what he wanted. I thought really it would help to save his life.'
> 'And it did?'
> 'No, it didn't.'
> 'Did he die?'
> 'No, but his life didn't need saving.' (chapter 16, pp. 115–116)

Elder's well-being was, in Daisy's mind, worth the risk. That it was achieved at considerable cost to her own security, and that her action made no appreciable difference to the intended beneficiary, does not enter into her calculations. Her basic faith in the potential for human happiness remains intact.

The same conviction informs her desire to ensure that Fred is happy on their walk, and to a lesser degree, her wish to rescue the Wrayburns from domestic chaos, to protect Kate the student nurse from exposing her incompetence and to make the best of her mother's shoplifting in Selfridges.

Professor Flowerdew's faith

Professor Flowerdew's case occupies the other end of the spectrum. Whereas Daisy believes in possibilities, without any tangible assurances, he is mistrustful of anything that cannot be observed.

Professor Flowerdew is confronting not just a difference in scientific
opinion, but a set of proposals that – were he to believe in them – would
collapse his orderly sense of the world he inhabits. His faith in the prin-
ciples of physics is his faith in general. This is poignantly illustrated in
Fred's interview with him at the beginning of the final chapter. Flowerdew has commissioned Fred to take notes at a lecture on Rutherford's
work, and it is with a sense of something like an ending that he thinks
about the future.

> Professor Flowerdew would never change his mind. That was not pos-
> sible for him. It was not that he supported J J Thomson's orderly atom
> against Rutherford's wild, airy and fractious one. To him, both these
> great intellects were pursuing nothings. Like Benedict XIII himself, he
> might be asked to admit defeat, but would never recognise it as legiti-
> mate, or even respectable. He might find it necessary to retreat even
> farther into seclusion. He might, even, have to apply for a post at
> Oxford, but if this should happen, Fred Fairly, his first assistant after
> all these years and, in a sense, his last throw, must on no account be
> asked to suffer. Some way must be devised so that Fairly would be able
> to continue at St Angelicus, unembarrassed and undistressed, for the
> rest of his natural life. (p. 162)

Fred's faith

Fred himself has a far more provisional attitude to the nature and order
of the world. We are given hints that he has become something of an
agnostic in his conversation with the Master, who asks him whether he
has 'made up [his] mind on the most important question of all' (p.12).

Fred immediately takes this to mean his religious beliefs, although this is not what the Master has in mind. (We will return to his question later.) Yet, as the anxious rehearsal in advance of a visit to his parents shows, Fred has not altogether lost his religious conviction:

> The best thing would be to explain at once that as from the beginning of the summer he was an unbeliever, but his unbelief was conditional. He had no acceptable evidence that Christianity was true, but he didn't think it impossible that at some point he might be given a satisfactory reason to believe in it. (p. 33)

It is Daisy who offers Fred a satisfactory reason to believe, though it would be straining the reading to say that she directs him back towards Christianity. At first, it appears that their strange meeting in a tangle of bicycles and carts presents a series of observable events that lead Fred to a logical conclusion. But to deduce from the circumstance of waking up next to her that he ought to marry her is a way of rationalising something that is not subject to rational laws at all: human love itself.

There are subtle hints of this at an early stage. We have already noted the Master's unfinished question in the first chapter about 'the most important question of all' (p. 12). Are we entitled to assume that the Master is referring to marriage, which would entail losing a position in St Angelicus? When Mr and Mrs Wrayburn call on Fred in hospital and report that the police are trying to trace Daisy, Fred's reaction is impatient. 'He didn't want Daisy traced. He wanted her found' (p. 58). But a much more telling piece of evidence comes much later, when Fred, distraught after the revelations of the trial, returns to conduct a tutorial for a group of students.

EXERCISE

📖 Re-read chapter 20 ('Fred's advice to his students', pp. 152–155).

Give careful consideration to his essay topic, which asks the class to design a rational system for measuring human happiness, and try to say what is faulty in the question. You may want to refer to the students' private reaction (p. 155).

Believing against the facts

The trial following the accident destroys everything that Fred depended on in his construction of Daisy. When it emerges that she may have delayed plans to spend the night with Kelly to the day after the accident, Fred is unable to adopt the stance he took at the Disobligers' Society and to argue against what he believes. His interview with Daisy at Dr Sage's hospital is hardly more reassuring. For once, there are laws in this misery, but they permit 'only a certain number of questions . . . Also, he was already asking the wrong ones' (p. 158). His one hope is that Daisy may have denied knowing Kelly in order to protect Fred's feelings, but even this consolation is unavailable. Instead, she seems more protective of Kelly, who is ageing and has dyed hair, and lacks Fred's educational advantages. This is the sober side of the game played by the Disobligers: arguing against one's beliefs is an arid occupation when it involves the realities of human lives. For 'now there seemed to be another law or regulation by which they were obliged to say to each other what they did not mean and to attack what they wished to defend' (p. 159).

It is this knowledge that distresses Daisy more than the dread of being found by Kelly as she leaves Mrs Wrayburn's house for the last time and meets Mrs Turner, who offers her a ride on the cart that caused the accident in the first place. Daisy 'was crying not from fear, but on account of the hurt she had done to Fred' (chapter 22, 'The Gate of Angels', p. 164). Mrs Turner's suspicion that Daisy has lost something points more to this loss than to the loss of any piece of luggage.

As Daisy is walking through Cambridge to the station, not quite sure of the way, the cry of the blind Master who has fallen over in the court of St Angelicus prompts her to enter the inexplicably open gate. Ignorant of the College's history and of its aversion to women on the premises, she applies her nursing skills amid the alarmed noises of the fellows and then leaves. 'The slight delay, however, meant that she met Fred Fairly walking slowly back to St Angelicus' (p. 167).

These events belong to the class of coincidence. At least, that is one interpretation. But *The Gate of Angels* has introduced us to another way of interpreting the world. It is, the novel suggests, not a place without system where human beings are helpless victims of the whims of fate. The appearance of chaos and disorder should not be discounted, because the events that overtake the characters undeniably have a strange and exaggerated aspect. Yet, with the reader's privileges of time and a larger view, we can see glimmers of resolution. That does not mean that the central figures are deprived of any power of self-determination, for the ending of the narrative is provisional. It is only a chance meeting, not a promise that Daisy and Fred will marry and live happily ever after. Equally, it is not a guarantee that the unsavoury Kelly will never be seen again. At the same time, it does propose that there is an inherent order in chaos, and that there can be human happiness, even if it will not submit to a rational system of measurement.

Faith and the tradition

We have approached this novel as a particular presentation of the workings of faith. In the process, we have seen that faith works in a number of different ways, although we have not noted all of them.

EXERCISE

At this stage, you may find if useful to think about the significance of the Master's blindness and about the contribution of Dr Matthews' ghost story to the unfolding of the tale.

A consistent motif has been the relationship of observation to belief. In the Second Letter to the Corinthians, Paul reminds his audience that 'we walk by faith and not by sight' (2 Corinthians 5:7). This is a principle that is lived out literally by the blind master, resisted entirely by Professor Flowerdew and in a sense theoretically adhered to by physicists who propose invisible subatomic particles. Fred comes to depend on his faith in Daisy over his powers of observation, as the trial scene makes especially clear.

Faith also exists in the form of a belief that circumstances and people are intrinsically capable of being transformed, even if the evidence is against this. The parables of Jesus contain many improbable challenges to faith. Jesus tells the disciples that faith the size of a grain of mustard seed can achieve astonishing feats (Matthew 17:20). The gospels tell the story of a storm on Lake Galilee which terrifies the disciples. Jesus calms the storm, but rebukes his companions for their lack of faith (Mark 4:40). The healing miracles consistently refer to the faith of those who recover as an important part of their physical transformation (for example Mark 5:34; 10:52; Luke 8:48; 17:19). This is the kind of faith we have traced in Daisy's career, notably as James Elder's nurse and in her compassion for Kelly.

Most important, however, is the place of faith among the three so-called theological virtues of faith, hope and love. In fact, faith works by love (the classical reference is 1 Corinthians 13). What the novel shows us in the end is that the three must exist together in order for human beings to be truly happy. The process of bringing them into synchrony is likely to be difficult and even painful, but faith also gives the power of endurance to carry those who possess it through to the end.

Further reading

Criticism

It is hard to find criticism of contemporary writers. Sometimes, it is better to read more novels by an author whose work you have sampled and enjoyed, and then to compare these with other writers.

Novels by Penelope Fitzgerald

Fitzgerald, P (1987), *Innocence*, London, Flamingo.
Fitzgerald, P (1988), *Offshore*, London, Flamingo.
Fitzgerald, P (1989), *The Bookshop*, London, Flamingo.
Fitzgerald, P (1989), *At Freddie's*, London, Flamingo.
Fitzgerald, P (1991), *The Gate of Angels*, London, Flamingo.
Fitzgerald, P (1994), *The Golden Child*, London, Flamingo.
Fitzgerald, P (1996), *The Beginning of Spring*, London, Flamingo.
Fitzgerald, P (1996), *The Blue Flower*, London, Flamingo.
Fitzgerald, P (1997), *Human Voices*, London, Flamingo.
(Other contemporary novelists who touch on similar religiously significant themes include: Beryl Bainbridge, Anita Brookner, Joanna Trollope and Penelope Lively.)

Useful background

Brooke, C N L (1993), *A History of the University of Cambridge*, vol. IV 1870-1990, Cambridge, Cambridge University Press. (See especially chapters 2 and 6.)
Cross, F L and Livingstone, E A (eds) (1997), *The Oxford Dictionary of the Christian Church*, Oxford, Oxford University Press (third edition). (See entry on 'faith'.)
Tilby, A (1992), *Science and the Soul*, London, SPCK.

REFERENCES

Abrams, M H (1999), *A Glossary of Literary Terms*, Fort Worth and London, Harcourt Brace, College (seventh edition).

Alter, R (1981), *The Art of Biblical Narrative*, London and Sydney, George Allen and Unwin.

Bal, M (1987), *Lethal Love: feminist literary readings of biblical love stories*, Bloomington and Indianapolis, Indiana University Press.

Blake, W (1977), *The Complete Poems*, ed. A Ostriker, Harmondsworth, Penguin.

Danielson, D (1989), The Fall of Man and Milton's theodicy, in D Danielson (ed.), *The Cambridge Companion to Milton*, pp. 113–129, Cambridge, Cambridge University Press.

Eliot, T S (1972), *Selected Essays*, London, Faber and Faber (third edition).

Honig, E (1959), *Dark Conceit: the making of allegory*, London, Faber and Faber.

Jackson, G (1986), *25 Domestic Sonnets*, Lincoln, Asgill Press.

Jackson, G (1995), *Charnal Supper*, Lincoln, Asgill Press.

Jasper, D (1992), *The Study of Literature and Religion: an introduction*, Basingstoke, Macmillan (second edition).

Johnson, S (1971), Cowley, in B H Bronson (ed.), *Samuel Johnson: Rasselas, poems and selected prose*, pp. 353–365, New York, Holt, Rinehart and Winston (third edition).

Josipovici, G (1988), *The Book of God: a response to the Bible*, New Haven, Connecticut and London, Yale University Press.

Prickett, S (1986), *Words and the Word: language, poetics and biblical interpretation*, Cambridge, Cambridge University Press.

Ricoeur, P (1975), The specificity of religious language, in *Semeia* 4, ed. J D Crossan, pp. 107–148.

Ryan, K (ed.) (1999), *Shakespeare: the last plays*, London and New York, Longman.

Sasson, J (1989), Ruth, in R Alter and F Kermode (eds), *The Literary Guide to the Bible*, pp. 320–329, London, Fontana.

Shewan, R (1977), *Oscar Wilde: art and egotism*, London, Macmillan.

The Book of Common Prayer, Cambridge, Cambridge University Press.

The New Jerusalem Bible (Study Edition) (1994), London, Darton, Longman and Todd.

GLOSSARY AND BIOGRAPHY

adjective a descriptive word, qualifying or amplifying the meaning of a noun (naming word).

adumbrate to foreshadow or bring into relief an idea or detail that has previously been in the background of a description or discussion.

allegory a narrative or description in which literal events are conveyed by sustained reference to a secondary structure of ideas or events.

alliteration repetition of a speech sound in a sequence of nearby words.

anachronism a displaced reference which relates things to a period of time to which they do not belong.

anthropomorphism giving human characteristics to other than human creatures.

Austen, Jane (1775–1817) a novelist whose works continue to be regarded as among the great achievements of English literature.

Blake, William (1757–1827) an engraver by training, Blake became a poet. He produced a great range of work, from lyric to mystical or prophetic writing, often with striking illustrations.

canon originally used of Scripture, the term refers to those books with an acknowledged and official place in the Old and New Testament sequences. In literature, **canon** refers to those works that might be said to constitute a core of material universally acknowledged as having a claim to a place in a tradition of excellence.

conceit a figure of speech establishing a striking parallel between two very different things or situations.

couplet two consecutive lines of verse with the same end-rhyme.

Dryden, John (1631–1700) poet and writer of tragicomedy.

Eliot, T(homas) S(tearns) (1888–1965) born in St Louis, Missouri, he settled in England in 1915. Eliot set a new tone in modern poetry, and exerted great influence as a literary and cultural critic.

eschatology the doctrine of the so-called last things – death, judgement, hell and heaven – and their effect upon the way human beings live their lives.

Herbert, George (1593–1633) writer of distinguished religious verse and usually included in the school of metaphysical poets.

homophone a word pronounced in the same way as another, but having a different spelling and meaning, for instance, *sail* and *sale*.

Hopkins, Gerard Manley (1844–1889) became a Jesuit novice in 1866, putting aside his poetry and only beginning to write again at the express request of his superior.

iconography illustration of a particular theme or subject using a visual medium such as painting or sculpture.

image a picture made of words.

irony ranges from a simple reversal of meaning to much more intricate usages. Structural irony will use events rather than words to achieve its effects.

Johnson, Samuel (1709–1784) critic and essayist, best known as the compiler of an English dictionary that became a standard work.

Langland, William (c.1330–1386) thought to have been a cleric in minor orders, lived in Malvern, Worcestershire.

Larkin, Philip (1922–1985) gifted lyric poet, openly scornful of positions of faith.

lyric a fairly short poem, consisting of the utterance of a single speaker.

metaphor ranges from similarity to more subtle ways of bringing concepts together so that they interact. Ordinary language is metaphorical by its nature.

metaphysical poetry a form of poetry in which abstract notions, for example love and religion, are vividly conveyed in colourful and often astonishing figures of speech.

metre any form of poetic rhythm.

Milton, John (1608–1674) began writing verse while a student at Cambridge. He was diverted into political pamphlets and at one time was imprisoned for his political stance.

octet or **octave** the first eight lines of a **Petrarchan sonnet**.

oxymoron a figure of speech which combines incongruous and apparently contradictory words and meanings for poetic effect.

paradox an apparently contradictory statement which, when inspected closely, turns out to contain a truth that brings opposites together.

parody imitative use of the words, style, attitudes and ideas of an author in such a way as to make them ridiculous; 'verbal cartoons'.

pathos a scene or passage designed to evoke feelings of tenderness, pity or sympathetic sorrow in the audience.

personification giving human and often embodied characteristics to a quality or abstraction.

Priestley, J(ohn) B(oynton) (1894–1984) born in Bradford. He wrote prolifically in a number of genres, but is best known as a novelist and playwright.

quatrain a group of four rhyming lines within a poem.

sestet the last six lines of a **Petrarchan sonnet**, following the **octet** or **octave**.

simile a figure of speech in which one thing is likened to another in such a way as to clarify and enhance an image using the words 'like' or 'as'. There is a strong case for claiming **simile** as a species of **metaphor**.

Shakespeare, William (1564–1616) the foremost English dramatist, having begun his career as an actor.

sonnet normally a fourteen-line poem. There are many variations in shape. The

Petrarchan or **Italian sonnet** (named from the Italian Renaissance poet Petrarch) has an **octave** or **octet** with the rhyme-scheme abba abba, followed by a **sestet** with the rhyme-scheme cde cde (or cdc dcd). The **Spenserian sonnet** (named from the sixteenth-century poet Edmund Spenser) has three **quatrains** rhyming abab bcbc cdcd, with a closing **couplet** rhyming ee. The Shakespearean sonnet has three **quatrains** rhyming abab cdcd efef, with a closing **couplet** rhyming gg.

stanza a group of lines of verse. It is a unit of structure in a poem, and has a pattern determined by the number of lines, their metre and their rhyme.

typology the technique of foreshadowing, or throwing into relief qualities and characteristics, or making links and connections between themes and persons.

Vaughan, Henry (1621–1695) religious poet whose work often displays powerful qualities of insight.

Watts, Isaac (1674–1748) nonconformist hymn-writer and poet.

Wilde, Oscar (1854–1900) Irish-born author of four comedies, short stories, poetry and literary criticism; a colourful figure convicted of gross indecency and sentenced to prison for two years in 1894.

Applying for the Church Colleges' Certificate Programme

The certificate programme is available in Anglican Church Colleges of Higher Education throughout England and Wales. There are currently hundreds of students on this programme, many with no previous experience of study of this kind. There are no entry requirements. Some people choose to take Certificate courses for their own interest and personal growth, others take these courses as part of their training for ministry in the church. Some go on to complete the optional assignments and, after the successful completion of three courses, gain the Certificate. Courses available through the *Exploring Faith: theology for life* series are ideal for establishing ability and potential for studying theology and biblical studies at degree level, and they provide credit onto degree programmes.

For further details of the Church Colleges' Certificate programme, related to this series, please contact the person responsible for Adult Education in your local diocese or one of the colleges at the addresses provided:

The Administrator of Part-time Programmes, Department of Theology and Religious Studies, Chester College, Parkgate Road, CHESTER, CH1 4BJ ☎ 01244 375444

The Registry, Roehampton Institute, Froebel College, Roehampton Lane, LONDON, SW15 5PJ ☎ 020 8392 3087

The Registry, Canterbury Christ Church University College, North Holmes Road, CANTERBURY, CT1 1QU ☎ 01227 767700

The Registry, College of St Mark and St John, Derriford Road, PLYMOUTH, PL6 8BH ☎ 01752 636892

The Registry, Trinity College, CARMARTHEN, Carmarthenshire, SA31 3EP ☎ 01267 676767

Church Colleges' Programme, The Registry, King Alfred's College, Sparkford Road, WINCHESTER, SO22 4NR ☎ 01962 841515

Part-time Programmes, The Registry, College of St Martin, Bowerham Road, LANCASTER, LA1 3JD ☎ 01524 384529